Brilliant HTML5 & CSS3

Josh Hill and James A Brannan

Prentice Hall
is an imprint of

Harlow, England • London • New York • Boston • San Francisco • Toronto • Sydney • Singapore • Hong Kong
Tokyo • Seoul • Taipei • New Delhi • Cape Town • Madrid • Mexico City • Amsterdam • Munich • Paris • Milan

Pearson Education Limited
Edinburgh Gate
Harlow CM20 2JE
United Kingdom
Tel: +44 (0)1279 623623
Fax: +44 (0)1279 431059
Website: www.pearsoned.co.uk

First published in Great Britain in 2011

ISBN: 978-0-273-74712-3

British Library Cataloguing-in-Publication Data
A catalogue record for this book is available from the British Library

Library of Congress Cataloging-in-Publication Data
Hill, Josh.
  Brilliant HTML5 & CSS3 / Josh Hill and James A Brannan.
      p. cm.
  ISBN 978-0-273-74712-3 (pbk.)
  1. Web sites--Design. 2. HTML (Document markup language) 3. Cascading style sheets. I. Brannan, James A. II. Title. III. Title: Brilliant HTML5 and CSS3.
  TK5105.888.H54 2011
  006.7'4--dc22
                            2011006097

Microsoft product screenshots reprinted with permission from Microsoft Corporation.
Adobe product screenshots reprinted with permission from Adobe Systems Incorporated.

10 9 8 7 6 5 4 3 2 1
15 14 13 12 11

Typeset in 11pt Arial Condensed by 30
Printed and bound in Great Britain by Scotprint, Haddington

Brilliant guides

What you need to know and how to do it

When you're working on your computer and come up against a problem that you're unsure how to solve or want to accomplish something in an application that you aren't sure how to do, where do you look? Manuals and traditional training guides are usually too big and unwieldy and are intended to be used as end-to-end training resources, making it hard to get to the info you need right away without having to wade through pages of background information that you just don't need at that moment – and helplines are rarely that helpful!

Brilliant guides have been developed to allow you to find the info you need easily and without fuss and guide you through the task using a highly visual, step-by-step approach – providing exactly what you need to know when you need it!

Brilliant guides provide the quick easy-to-access information that you need, using the Contents and Troubleshooting guide to help you find exactly what you need to know, then presenting each task in a visual manner. Numbered steps then guide you through each task or problem, using numerous screenshots to illustrate each step. Added features include 'Cross reference …' boxes that point you to related tasks and information in the book, while 'Did you know?…' sections alert you to relevant expert tips, tricks and advice to further expand your skills and knowledge.

In addition to covering all major office PC applications, and related computing subjects, the *Brilliant* series also contains titles that will help you in every aspect of your working life, such as writing the perfect CV, answering the toughest interview questions and moving on in your career.

Brilliant guides are the light at the end of the tunnel when you are faced with any minor or major task.

Author's acknowledgements

In working on a book like this, it's always a challenge to know where all the information comes from when it comes together, but for me, I have to first acknowledge James Brannan, who put together the first edition of *Brilliant HTML & CSS* in 2009 and give special thanks to Katy Robinson and Steve Temblett at Pearson for choosing me to do this update. I'd also like to acknowledge my agent, Neil Salkind from The Salkind Agency, and StudioB, who all work tirelessly to tolerate me, explain the ins and outs of publishing and hold my hand and soothe me when I need it. I also wish to thank the many sources of information cited within the book for their incredible resources, such as the WHATWG, Veign.com and FreeCSSTemplates. I couldn't have written this book without their help.

Dedication

To my patient and loving wife, and constant first reader, Vanessa. I couldn't do anything without you there to support, guide and encourage me. Thank you.

About the author

Josh Hill is a technical supervisor, technical author and editor and fiction writer, living in northeastern Illinois. When he isn't working, writing or editing, he enjoys spending time with his daughter Victoria, his son Joshua and his wife Vanessa, provided the weather permits.

Publisher's acknowledgements

We are grateful to the following for permission to reproduce copyright material:

Screenshots

Screenshots on pages 6, 13, 180, 201 from Notepad++, available under the GNU General Public License (http://www.gnu.org/licenses/gpl-2.0.html); Screenshots on pages 6, 11, 13, 15, 21, 23, 25, 27, 29, 32, 37, 41, 46, 49, 51, 54, 57, 66, 71, 72, 74, 76, 79, 85, 87, 94, 96, 100, 102, 104, 106, 108, 111, 113, 120, 122,

Contents

Introduction

Welcome to *Brilliant HTML5 & CSS3*, a visual quick reference guide that will teach you all that you need to know to create clean, forward-looking, standards-compliant, accessible websites using HyperText Markup Language & Cascading Style Sheets. It will give you a solid grounding on the theory, coding skills and best practices needed to use HTML5 & CSS3 to build sophisticated web pages – a complete reference for the beginner and intermediate user.

Find what you need to know – when you need it

You don't have to read this book in any particular order. We've designed it so that you can jump in, get the information you need and jump out. To find what you need, just look up the task in the Contents or Troubleshooting guide and turn to the page listed. Read the text or follow the step-by-step instructions and look at the illustrations, and you're done.

How this book works

Each task is presented with step-by-step instructions in one column and screenshots in the other. This arrangement lets you focus on a single task without having to turn the pages too often.

How you'll learn

Find what you need to know – when you need it

How this book works

Step-by-step instructions

Troubleshooting guide

Spelling

Step-by-step instructions

This book provides concise step-by-step instructions that show you how to accomplish a task. Each set of instructions includes illustrations that directly correspond to the easy-to-follow steps. Eye-catching text features provide additional helpful information in bite-sized chunks to help you work more efficiently or teach you more in-depth information. The 'For your information' features provide tips and techniques to help you work smarter, while the 'Cross reference' boxes lead you to other parts of the book containing related information about the task. Essential information is highlighted in 'Important' boxes that will ensure you don't miss any vital suggestions and advice.

Troubleshooting guide

This book offers quick and easy ways to diagnose and solve common problems that you might encounter in the Troubleshooting guide. The problems are grouped into categories that follow the order of the chapters.

Spelling

We have used UK spelling conventions throughout this book. You may therefore notice some inconsistencies between the text and the software on your computer, which is likely to have been developed in the USA. We have, however, adopted US spelling for the words 'disk' and 'program', as these are commonly accepted throughout the world.

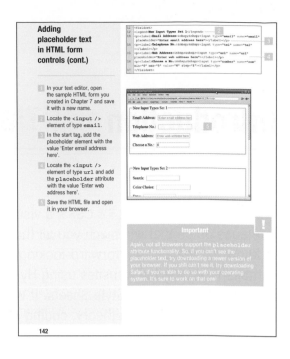

Adding placeholder text in HTML form controls (cont.)

1 In your text editor, open the sample HTML form you created in Chapter 7 and save it with a new name.

2 Locate the `<input />` element of type email.

3 In the start tag, add the placeholder element with the value 'Enter email address here'.

4 Locate the `<input />` element of type url and add the placeholder attribute with the value 'Enter web address here'.

5 Save the HTML file and open it in your browser.

Important

Again, not all browsers support the placeholder attribute functionality. So, if you can't see the placeholder text, try downloading a newer version of your browser. If you still can't see it, try downloading Safari, if you're able to do so with your operating system. It's sure to work on that one!

142

Troubleshooting guide

Introduction to HTML

Introduction

HTML stands for Hyper Text Markup Language. HTML is not a computer programming language. HTML is a markup language, which puts instructions, or tags, around text so an Internet browser knows how to display the text on the screen. It's a set of instructions for the web browser. For example, this tag:

```
<b>Text to display on screen</b>
```

tells the web browser to show the text between the `<b>` and `</b>` tags as bold type.

There are many free tools available to help you write standards-compliant HTML for web pages. Some tools are so sophisticated you don't need to know much HTML or CSS at all, such as Adobe's Dreamweaver. Apple computers come with programs to build point-and-click, drag-and-drop web pages. Simple, easy and effective ... until you need to deviate from the template, customise the page or do something outside the command set from the menus. Then, you'll need to know HTML and CSS. While these tools are great and make building web pages simple and fun, you can build them by hand and have more control over how your web pages look and behave. All you need is a good text editor, a web browser to test your results and a little patience.

HTML5 is the latest HTML iteration and now includes functionality for HTML which, previously, had to be done in other markup or scripting languages. It has also deprecated, or phased out, some earlier functionality. CSS, covered later in

What you'll do

Gather equipment – text editors and web browsers

Make sense of HTML – elements, tags and attributes

Learn about the basic structure of an HMTL page

Create your first HTML document, with declarations, header, metadata and title

Find out about HTML comments

this book, is far more effective at controlling how a web page looks, while HTML5 focuses on page structure rather than appearance.

While learning HTML and CSS will certainly help you on your way to becoming a web designer and/or developer, there are many other things you need to know which fall beyond the scope of this book. Scripting and programming languages, database connections, dynamic and active content and many other things aren't covered here. What you will learn here will make you a competent and confident handler of HTML and CSS, however, which is a good starting point.

If you're already familiar with how to edit, view and save HTML documents, you can skim through this chapter and move on to other things. If not, this chapter will help to prepare you for tasks covered in subsequent chapters. You'll learn how to use the basic tools you'll need – a browser and a text editor – and some other tools to help you write HTML documents. To do any of the tasks which follow, you'll need to know how to mark up text and how to load the file into a web browser to view the results. There are finished examples you can use to check your work and help you along the way. As with all *Brilliant* series books, the steps you need to take are clearly set out and numbered to help you at each stage.

As stated in the Introduction, creating HTML pages doesn't require much equipment. All you need is a computer, of course, an Internet web browser, such as Internet Explorer or Mozilla Firefox, and a text editor, such as Notepad. With these few items, you can create any web page imaginable. We will also create a file folder to store your completed files. To ensure the success of your tasks, make sure you have all these things ready to create an HTML document.

Gathering equipment – text editors and web browsers

1

Important

The line numbers you see on screenshots of HTML documents are a function of the text editor; do *not* type them in! (See the screenshot for step 4 of the task for an example of these line numbers.)

Important

Don't confuse text editors with word processor software or even rich text editors! There are critical differences. Many modern word processors can create HTML documents from text, but they include many hidden codes which can create problems for some browsers. Rich text editors do not add as much formatting, but do have some and are not designed for creating HTML documents. Text editors have no formatting capabilities and do not add any extra code to created documents.

Did you know?

Most operating systems, such as Windows, Linux or Mac OSX, come with text editors. You can also download free text editors which enhance their functionality and can assist you with writing HTML documents. For this book, I used Notepad++, which is an enhanced, free piece of text- and code-editing software (you can download Notepad++ at: **http://notepad-plus-plus.org**). Most of the screenshots of the text editor in this book are of Notepad++.

Gathering equipment – text editors and web browsers (cont.)

Timesaver tip

Your computer is probably set up to open HTML documents using the default web browser. Just double-clicking any file with the extension .html or .htm will cause the file to open in the web browser specified as the default.

2

Be sure the file type selected is HTML when saving an HTML file in a text editor.

1 Decide on a text editor to use. Most computers come with a built-in, or default, text editor. In Windows, the default text editor is Notepad. Whichever text editor you decide on is also known as the HTML editor.

2 Create a folder to save your HTML files to when you've completed each task. I generally do this on the desktop for convenience, but you can create it anywhere you'd like.

3 Identify the browser you use to view Internet pages. You are most likely familiar and comfortable with the default browser your computer uses. So long as you know how to open and view files in the web browser of your choice, any of them will work fine.

Gathering equipment – text editors and web browsers (cont.)

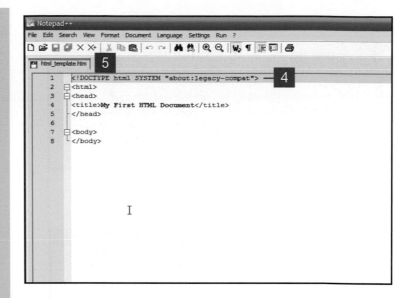

4 Open the text editor you'll use for the tasks in this book and type the information shown in the screenshot. This is the Document Type Declaration or DOCTYPE Declaration or DTD. The HTML, head and body tags for an HTML document, which are all mandatory tags, are also included. Tags and HTML structure will be discussed later in this chapter.

5 Save the newly created document as html_template. htm. This template will be used for several of the tasks in later chapters.

6 Open the template file in your browser window. You should see a blank screen with the title My First HTML Document across the title bar at the top of the screen.

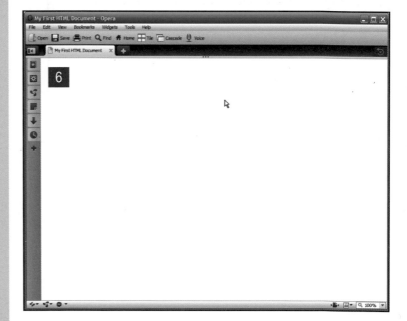

For your information

The World Wide Web Consortium, or W3C, is a worldwide governing body for Internet standards. While the W3C has no legal authority, it does provide an overall standards compliance platform for companies which produce software and languages for the Internet. Its members include companies such as Microsoft, Apple, IBM, Hewlett-Packard and others. The W3C brings these major companies together to negotiate agreements on recommended changes and inclusions for Internet-specific languages and technologies, such as HTML, CSS and web browsers. It has the compiled standards, recommended revisions and general current state of most web technologies. Visit its website (at: **www.w3.org**) to see the latest changes to HTML and CSS.

7 Locate some additional online resources and bookmark them. Start by bookmarking the World Wide Web Consortium's website (at: **www.w3.org**). Also bookmark W3Schools' website (at: **http://w3schools.org**), and the Web Design Group's (WDG) site (at: **http://htmlhelp.com**).

8 Download the free quick reference guides, available from Veign (at: **www.veign. com/reference/index.php**), for both HTML5 and CSS3.

Making sense of HTML – elements, tags and attributes

HTML is a markup language composed of various parts. Those parts are tags, elements and attributes.

HTML tags are instructions to browsers about the content of an element. For instance, here is an HTML element which tells the browser to display the text between the tags as a paragraph:

```
<p>Text content of the element</p>
```

Tags are composed of angle brackets with markup instructions between them. In the example above, the letter '**p**' surrounded by angle brackets is the paragraph tag. The first tag is the start tag and it tells the browser to display all the text that follows as a paragraph. The tag with '**/p**' in angle brackets is the end tag. This tells the browser the end of the paragraph has been reached. The forward slash means 'end' in HTML tags.

HTML elements are composed of a start tag, content and an end tag. Things such as headings, paragraphs and tables are elements.

Did you know?

HTML5 does not require single or double quotes around attribute values. Older markup languages do, however, so it is good practice to use them when marking up your HTML documents.

Attributes are specific properties of a tag. They define its behaviour or appearance. Many HTML tag attributes can be adjusted to alter the display. Attributes are listed in start tags only. To ensure compatibility with older HTML or XHTML versions, the attribute value is placed in single or double quotes, as here:

```
<img src="http://somelinktoapicture.
com/"></img>
```

For your information

HTML tags and elements are terms which have distinct meanings, but are interchangeable in common usage. Most web designers and developers do not distinguish between tags and elements anymore. Both terms are used interchangeably in this book as well.

The image tag – **<img>** – in the example above has a required attribute of **src** (source), which specifies the location of the image to be displayed.

HTML documents have a basic structure to them which is universal, no matter how simple or complex the web page appears onscreen. Some basic elements common to all HTML documents create that structure. Those basic elements include the Document Type Declaration (DTD), HTML element, head element and body element – all of which we put into our HTML template in the previous task.

The basic document structure has nothing to do with the page content, so don't be confused by this. Content is what we see on a page, but that has nothing to do with the basic structure of an HTML document. An HTML document's composition is partly visible and partly invisible to the viewer looking at a web page.

All HTML documents have two primary sections: the header and body. All the content of the page – everything that you see and interact with – is in the body. The header section contains data which is *not* visible – content the user or viewer doesn't actually see.

The first line of every HTML document, regardless of whatever else is included, must be the Document Type Declaration, also called the DOCTYPE Declaration or DTD. In earlier versions of HTML, many layers of adjustment and tweaking of HTML standards meant complex and difficult DTDs were required. With HTML5, however, the DTD is exceedingly simple. It must read as follows:

```
<!DOCTYPE html>
```

This DTD will work with earlier versions of HTML which might be encountered on web pages, too. The DTD tells the browser to expect an HTML document instead of another markup language or other type of document. Because of the DTD's function, there must be no white space – that is, blank lines – before the DTD. This is critical because if the browser encounters a blank line before the DTD, it will behave as though there is no DTD and the results may be unpredictable.

Basic structure of an HTML document

Basic structure of an HTML document (cont.)

After the DTD comes the HTML element. There is a start tag and an end tag to the HTML element, so it looks like this:

```
<html></html>
```

All other elements of the HTML file will be contained in this element, which tells the browser this is the HTML document.

The next section of the header is the head element, contained within the HTML element. It also has a start and an end tag:

```
<head></head>
```

The head section contains information about the document itself, such as its title (which will show in the title bar at the top of the browser), any metadata and any styles or scripts used in the document.

Next in line is the body section. This is the visible and interactive content of the document. Everything you can see on a web page goes in this section of the document. All the content and formatting of that content goes in the body section of the document.

Important

Make sure there are no blank lines in your HTML file before the DTD! This is *crucial!* Your web page may not behave as expected if a browser encounters a blank line before it encounters the DTD.

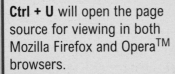

Timesaver tip

Ctrl + U will open the page source for viewing in both Mozilla Firefox and Opera™ browsers.

For your information

The HTML element is not mandatory in HTML5. In fact, the head and body elements are also optional. It's good practice to use them for code clarity and maintaining good standards, but they are not required elements of an HTML5 page.

For your information

The rest of the body of the HTML file or web page is contained in the HTML element. Finding the end tag may involve scrolling a long way down towards the bottom of the screen and there could be many other types of web page elements, too – scripts and programming items for example – but these are beyond the scope of this book.

Timesaver tip

Use the **Search** or **Find** feature in your browser to locate the tags as you look for them, if the browser allows it. This will speed up the process of finding the various elements.

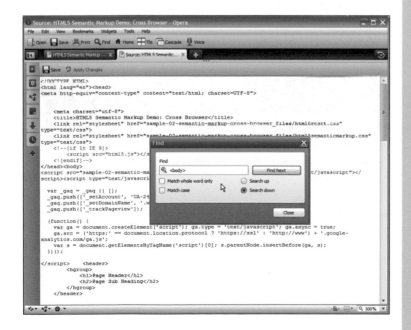

1. Open your web browser and navigate to your favourite website.
2. View the page source with your browser's **View Page Source** function. In Mozilla Firefox, go to **View**, **Page Source**; in Opera™, go to **View**, **Source**; in Internet Explorer, go to **View**, **Source**.
3. Identify the DTD. If one is used, it will be the very first line of the document.
4. Next, find the HTML element of the document. This will be somewhere after the DTD. Look for the opening tag only at first as the end tag will be at the very end of the document.
5. Look for the `<head>`, `<title>` and `<body>` elements of the page. On a busy, professional website, there are sure to be many other elements on the page as well.
6. Now locate the `<body>` element on the web page. Inside the `<body>` element will be all the visible parts of the web page – everything you see on the page is contained in the `<body>` element of the HTML document. Do not be surprised if the `<body>` tag is located fairly far down on the HTML document.

Introduction to HTML 11

Creating your first HTML document, with declarations, header, metadata and title

1. Open your HTML template – the one we made earlier in this chapter.

2. Save the template with a new name.

3. Click the mouse to place the cursor between the `<title>` and `</title>` tags. This is later referred to as putting the cursor in the title element.

4. Notice the `<title>` element is contained in the `<head>` element – that is, between the `<head>` and `</head>` tags.

5. Give the new web page a title. Make sure you give it a meaningful title. For instance, 'My first web page' is not as descriptive and useful as 'Josh Hill's first sample web page'. I would use the latter as my title.

In the last task, you examined a web page (or more, if you chose to) and deciphered the major sections of an HTML document – the `<header>` and `<body>` sections.

In this task, you will create your first HTML document. While, technically, you did this earlier by creating the HTML template, here you will add content to the web page and view it in your web browser. You will also add a title to the heading section of the HTML file and content to the body section and element.

Important

Be sure to make the new filename something that is meaningful to you. For instance, 'task1.html' may not be as helpful as 'chapter1webpage.html' later on.

Table 1.1 Tags used in this task

Tag	Function
`<!DOCTYPE.../>`	Specifies the document type declaration.
`<html></html>`	Specifies the HTML markup portion of a document.
`<head></head>`	Specifies an HTML document's header section or element.
`<title></title>`	Specifies the HTML document's title.
`<body></body>`	Specifies the HTML document's content section or element.

The results of this task are very straightforward. You will add a title to the `<title>` element which displays in the title bar in the web browser. You will also add content to the `<body>` element which then displays in the browser window.

For your information

The `<title>` element content is what will appear in the title bar in the browser when the web page has loaded.

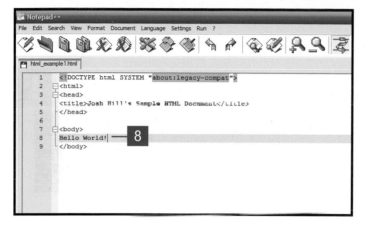

6 Place the cursor in the `<body>` element – that is, between the `<body>` and `</body>` tags.

7 Notice the `<body>` element comes after the `</head>` tag – that is, it comes after the `<head>` element.

8 Type 'Hello World!' in the `<body>` element, then save and close the sample web page HTML document.

9 Open the sample HTML page in your web browser. You should see the content you added in the `<body>` element on the main part of the screen and the title you added in the web page title bar.

For your information

If you use a tabbed interface browser (most of them are now), you will notice that the title you put in the `<title>` element of your sample HTML document will also appear as the title of the tab on which the page opens.

HTML comments

Comments in HTML, as in many other computer languages, are used to annotate the markup code. HTML comments are ignored by web browsers and not displayed. General practice, therefore, is to insert items not intended to be viewed in them. Browsers can still *act* on code in comments without showing it. This makes comments useful for code notations, hiding scripts and style elements from older browsers which do not understand them and would display them as plain text otherwise, and other things not meant to be shown onscreen. This way, scripts still run and style elements are still applied, but the code is hidden from view.

An HTML comment has an opening angle bracket, just like all other tags, followed by an exclamation mark. The exclamation mark is then followed by two hyphens. Any comment text, script data, style code or annotations of any kind are then added. The comment text is then followed by another pair of dashes and the closing angle bracket, like this:

```
<!-- This is an HTML comment -->
```

There is no limit to how many lines you can put in an HTML comment. This means you can place a great deal of script, style or notation information in them.

This task is very simple. You will create an HTML comment in the `<body>` element of your sample page and open it in a browser to see the comment does not show onscreen.

For your information

Many web pages include Cascading Style Sheet (CSS) code in the heading of an HTML document to prevent it from showing in the display. Older browsers still recognise the `<head>` element as information which is not displayed, and do not show it. Many scripts are also placed inside the `<head>` element, before the `<title>` element, of HTML documents.

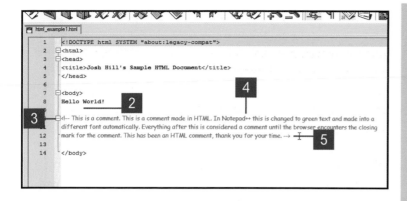

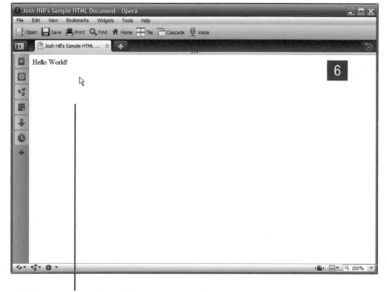

Note, none of the comment text is visible on the web page.

1 Open the sample web page you made in the last task in your text editor.

2 In the `<body>` element, click on a blank line and create a few more blank lines by pressing the **Enter** key two or three times.

3 In the middle of the white space, type the opening comment marker `<!--`.

4 Type a few remarks until you have several lines of text. Alternatively, write one sentence and copy it over and over.

5 At the end of the comment, type the closing comment marker `-->`.

6 Save the sample web page and open it in your web browser.

! Important

Despite their similarity in appearance, the opening and closing for an HTML comment aren't called tags. You can think of them as tags, though, as both start and end markers are required.

HTML comments (cont.)

Web page structure with HTML5 tags

Introduction

With earlier versions of HTML, placing elements on a page's `<body>` could be tricky. The elements themselves could also be limiting. For instance, in very early versions of HTML, tables were commonly used to place particular elements on a page. Each cell of the table was used as a different container for information. Later, framesets were permitted by HTML code and each frame on a page held different content.

HTML4.0 introduced the `<div>` tag, which was a generic division or container to hold information. The containing element could then be placed on the page and have special styling applied to it. This offered much greater control and nicer looking web pages, to be sure, but it still wasn't a solid structural framework.

HTML5 offers new tags which provide strong structural content for pages. Elements can be placed without resorting to styling control, so that HTML again becomes the markup for structuring and constructing a page. In other words, HTML5 allows the markup to be about page *construction* and the style component to be about how the page looks.

The trade-off for this stronger construction is that greater onus is placed on CSS for appearance and style considerations. Many of the inline formatting elements of HTML have been lost, or deprecated, so they are outmoded. The gain, however, is cleaner, more concise and more clearly readable code in the markup and greater structural capabilities than ever before.

What you'll do

Add HTML sections

Add HTML articles

Create HTML navigation

Create an HTML sidebar

Create an HTML content header

Create an HTML footer

Important

The `<div></div>` element is still a widely used and accepted content division element and will still be a valid tag in web development.

Now the generic `<div>` element is outmoded and more accurate, understandable tags have replaced it.

In this chapter, we examine some of the structural tags and see how they help us with our web page construction. We explore creating page sections and look at some HTML tag attributes to get a feel for what elements can do before we resort to CSS for style and appearance considerations.

For your information

Just because a tag, attribute or element is deprecated doesn't mean that HTML5-compliant browsers will fail to display them correctly. Deprecation means the tag or attribute has been either replaced by a new HTML tag, attribute or element or the function has been moved to CSS or scripting language support instead.

The `<section>` element creates a section in an HTML document and on a web page. The section can group content by theme or as part of an application or form. Sections usually have a header and can sometimes have a footer (these will be covered in more detail later in this chapter).

Table 2.1 Tag used in this task

Tag	Function
`<section>`... `</section>`	Creates a section in the body of an HTML document.

HTML document sections are created using the `<section>` tag, which requires both a start and an end tag:

```
<section>...</section>
```

HTML sections allow you to group related content together without having to use a generic `<div>` tag. For example, a web page might have articles in one section, advertising in another and a site map in yet another. Each section might have its own header and footer.

The `<section>` element can also be nested, meaning a section can be subdivided into further sections using more `<section></section>` tags. Each subsection can also have its own header and footer.

The results of this task are simple. You will add sections to a sample web page and an inline style to make the section distinguishable. The techniques for making the sections clearer with CSS are discussed more fully later in the book. You will be able to see two different lines of text in two different colours in your browser window, each as a separate section.

Adding HTML sections

2

Important

There are other grouping elements, such as the `<article>` and `<aside>` elements, which are covered later in this chapter. Most of the elements grouped together will be grouped thematically. All articles will be grouped together, any asides or sidebars will be grouped together and so on.

Adding HTML sections (cont.)

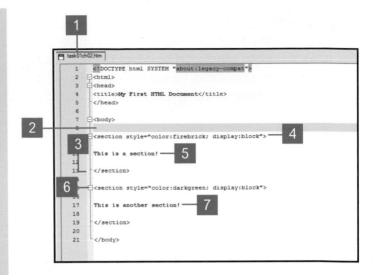

1. Open the HTML template you created in Chapter 1 in your text editor and save it with a new name.

2. Add a few blank lines in the `<body>` element.

3. In the `<body>` element, insert a `<section>` element with a start tag and an end tag on two different lines, that is, `<section>` and `</section>`.

4. In the `<section>` start tag (`<section>`), insert a space after the word 'section' and type the following inline style, all in lower-case letters:

   ```
   style="color:
   firebrick;
   display:block"
   ```

5. Type 'This is a section!' between the start and end tags.

6. Add another blank line or two and create another `<section>` element with a start tag and an end tag on two separate lines. Add the same inline style to the start tag as in step 4 above, but change the colour to 'darkgreen'.

Important

The line you add to the section tag in step 4 is a `style` attribute and here it changes the section's text colour. Normally, this will be done in CSS rather than inline. It is included as an inline style here to make the sections distinguishable on the screen.

Jargon buster

Inline style – A CSS style which is applied directly to the line or element it will affect (CSS is covered in detail from Chapter 10 onwards).

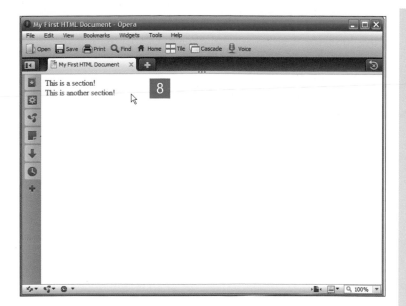

Adding HTML sections (cont.)

7 Add the text 'This is another section!' to the second `<section>` element.

8 Save the HTML file, then open it in your browser. Notice the two lines of text in the browser window are different colours. Each line represents a separate section in the HTML document.

For your information

The red and green text lines on the web page are on different lines because the `display:block` style command allows each element to be on its own line with no other elements beside it (this is explained more fully in the CSS portion of the book, from Chapter 10 onwards).

Adding HTML articles

Besides `<section>` elements, HTML provides other ways to divide the structure of a page. One of them is the `<article>` element.

The `<article>` element divides a page or site into discrete articles or items, such as forum and blog posts. The `<article>` element is an independent bit of content of any kind, really.

Table 2.2 Tag used in this task

Tag	Function
`<article>…` `</article>`	Creates an HTML article division on the site, web page or in an HTML document.

The `<article>` element has both a start and an end tag. While the `<section>` element groups thematic content, the `<article>` element is for a separate and distinct bit of information on the page or in a section or document. A `<section>` element can be used to subdivide an `<article>`, for instance, and `<article>` elements can be used to subdivide a section into discrete articles for a magazine- or newspaper-style web page layout.

One of the best ways to think about whether or not an `<article>` element or `<section>` element should be used is to decide if the content will make sense on its own in a feed reader. If so, it's an article. If not, then is the content related by a theme somehow? If so, a `<section>` element will work well.

This task is very simple. You will add articles to your sample web page and display it in the browser. You will keep each article on its own line with the addition of the `display:block` CSS style property in the start tag of the `<article>` element.

Important

Many HTML5 elements are not fully visible without using some CSS to highlight them (CSS is covered in more detail from Chapter 10 onwards).

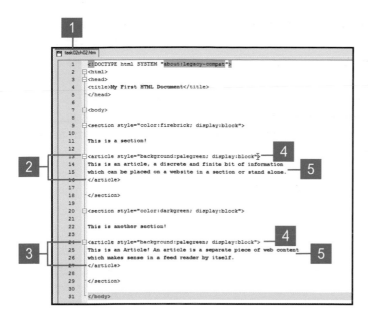

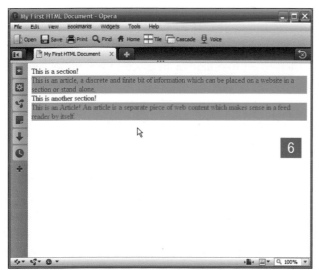

1 Open the web page you created in the last task using your text editor and save it with a new name.

2 In the first `<section>` element, add the `<article>` element's start and end tags: `<article>` and `</article>`.

3 Add an `<article>` element to the second section the same way.

4 In the start tag for both articles, add the following inline style: `style="background: palegreen; display:block"`

5 Between the `<article>` element tags, add some text to each article. Make the text unique to each article so they can be distinguished easily.

6 Save the HTML file and open it in your web browser.

Timesaver tip

If you've left your browser window open to your HTML documents, you can see the changes you make in many browsers by using the **Reload** or **Refresh** feature. In Mozilla Firefox and Internet Explorer, the command is **Ctrl + F5**. In SeaMonkey and Opera™, it's **Ctrl + R**. It can also be found in the menu system, usually on the **View** menu.

Creating HTML navigation

With earlier HTML versions, site navigation had to be created using available tags and the wits of the site designer and programmer. With HTML5, however, new elements are available which make creating site navigation easy and simple.

The **<nav>** element is a specific element for providing a section of primary links and a navigation area. CSS properties can be applied directly to the **<nav>** tag to give it the look and feel desired, rather than having to wrap it in a generic **<div>** element. The **<nav>** element has both a start and an end tag.

Table 2.3 Tag used in this task

Tag	Function
<nav>...</nav>	Creates an HTML site navigation division.

For your information

While the **<nav>** element is designed for use with site navigational links, other links and sidebar data can be placed in it as well. Like all other HTML elements, the contents are up to the site designer.

The results of this task are straightforward. You will add a navigational section to the sample web page you created earlier and add placeholder text to mark it visibly on the page.

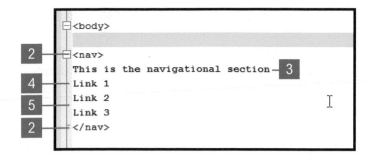

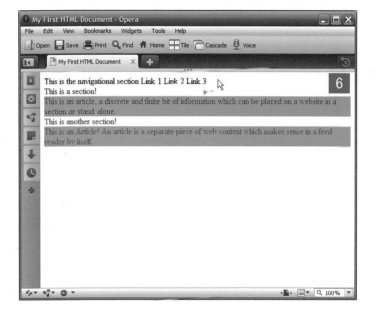

1 Open your sample web page in your text editor and save it with a new name.

2 In the `<body>` element, but before the first `<section>` element, add the `<nav>` element, using the `<nav>` and `</nav>` tags.

3 Between the `<nav>` tags, type 'This is the navigational section' and press **Enter**.

4 On a separate line, type 'Link 1' (no quotes), then press **Enter**.

5 Type 'Link 2' and 'Link 3' – without quotation marks – each on its own line.

6 Save the HTML file and open it in your browser.

Did you know?

Even though you placed each link text on a separate line, the web browser displayed all the links on the same line. That is because we didn't issue any instructions for the browser to show them on different lines and the web browser doesn't recognise the **Enter** key as a line break. HTML has several ways to do this and we'll show you them in the next chapter.

For your information

Not all tags in HTML have a start and end tag. All structural elements, however, do require both a start and an end tag to demarcate where the structure starts and ends and what is encompassed within it.

Creating an
HTML sidebar

You've probably noticed that, on many web pages, content isn't limited to just a single section down the middle of the page. There are sidebars on both sides and sometimes they house navigational aids, as we learned in the last task. Other times, sidebar content is *related* to the main content, but can also stand alone. Such sidebars can be built into the structure of web pages now with the `<aside>` element in HTML5.

The `<aside>` element has a start and an end tag and creates a sidebar section for a page. The name implies the kind of aside often found in print media, but it can also be a section where widgets and other links of interest can be placed, similar to a `<nav>` element.

Table 2.4 Tag used in this task

Tag	Function
`<aside>...</aside>`	Creates an HTML sidebar on a web page or in an HTML document.

The results of this task are simple. You will add an `<aside>` element to your sample web page and, like all the other structural elements in HTML, you can assign it specific formatting with CSS to make the sidebar look as you like. In this instance, we will create the aside without formatting, but will apply it in Chapter 3.

Important

While there are similarities between the `<aside>` and `<nav>` elements, it becomes important to delineate their uses and keep the coding segregated when designing and coding web pages. Others who look at the page structurally and examine the code should be able to make sense of the decisions the original designer made. So, use the `<nav>` element for site navigation or links to other documents and keep the `<aside>` element for the sidebar and its tangentially related content, as a matter of good practice.

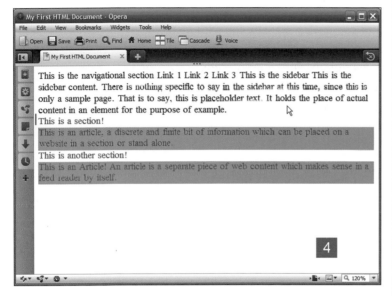

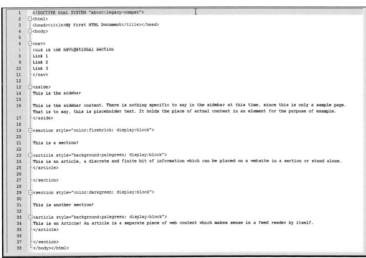

1 Open your sample web page in your text editor and save it with a new name.

2

2 In the `<body>` tag, under the `<nav>` element, after 'Link 3', add the `<aside>` element start and end tags — `<aside>` and `</aside>`.

3 Between the `<aside>` element tags, type 'This is the sidebar' (without quotes) and add some text. Make sure that there is at least one paragraph in the element.

4 Save the HTML file and open it in your web browser. The results are a little messy, but can be cleaned up easily later with CSS.

For your information

The content may seem a little confusing right now, but the HTML document you're creating should make things very clear. You can see this in the screenshot of the HTML document I've assembled along the way to serve as a guide for you.

Creating an HTML content header

!

Important

Do not confuse a *header* element with a *heading* element. The names may look alike and aren't always easy to tell apart, but they are very different. A header is a section of an HTML document or web page, while a heading is formatting applied to specific content. Headings are covered in Chapter 3.

Headers for sections, articles and even `<aside>` elements and `<nav>` sections are created using the `<header>` element. The `<header>` element usually defines a section of headings and subheadings.

There's nothing fancy to learn about headers. They're sections you place on your page to allow for headings. Like all structural HTML5 elements, they require a start and an end tag and can have their own formatting applied.

Table 2.5 Tag used in this task

Tag	Function
`<header>...</header>`	Creates an HTML header section on a web page or in a section or an article element.

In general, a `<header>` element will contain at least one heading element. Sectioning elements, however, don't go inside the `<header>` element and a heading element does not have to be inside a `<section>` element, though it typically is.

In this task, you will create two HTML `<header>` sections – one for the page itself and another for one of the articles on your sample web page. The results are straightforward and we will add a little CSS inline styling to help us distinguish the `<header>` from the rest of the page.

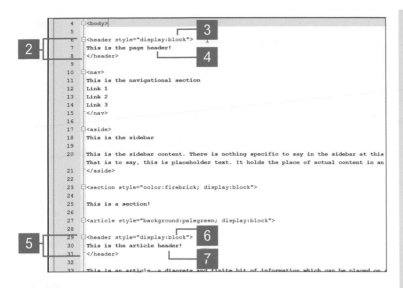

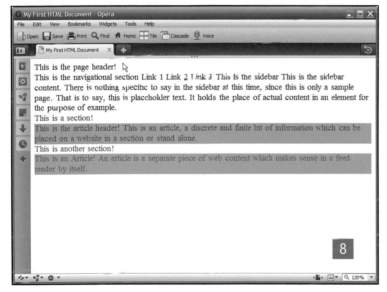

1 In your text editor, open the sample web page you made earlier and save it with a new name.

2 In the `<body>` element, above the `<nav>` element, add the start and end tags for the `<header>` element `<header>` and `</header>`.

3 In the start tag, add this inline style: `style= "display:block"`.

4 Between the tags type 'This is the page header!', without the quotes.

5 After the start tag of the first `<article>` element of your HTML document, add another `<header>` element.

6 Add the same inline CSS style as in step 3 above.

7 Between the tags type 'This is the article header!', without quotation marks.

8 Save the HTML file in your text editor and open it in your web browser.

Creating an
HTML content
header (cont.)

Important

The `style="display:block"` property allows the element to display in the box method and be on its own line in your browser window. We're doing this for visual clarity at this stage, but if you'd like to add the command to the `<nav>` element or the sidebar `<aside>` element, go ahead. Experiment with it so you can make sense of your web page visually. More detail on this will come when we get to CSS in Chapter 10.

For your information

HTML5 allows heading content to be grouped together so that browsers see headings, subheadings, alternative text and tag lines as single heading content in a single wrapping element on the summary or outline level. A heading is lumped together with its subheading or tag line and only the highest heading level shows in outline or summary. There is no impact on how the heading looks on the page, only on how the browser handles the group in summary or outline view. The grouped headings show as the highest level of heading in the `<hgroup>` element only, whether it's the `<h1>` element or the `<h6>` element. To have any impact, there must be more than one heading element within the hgroup. The `<hgroup>` element requires a start and an end tag – `<hgroup>` and `</hgroup>`.

You can create a footer section in your HTML document. Its content could be the navigational aids found at the bottom of many web pages, along with a contact link and a link to information about the company or person the website belongs to or else it could be the web designer's name and a link back to his or her web page. It could be anything, but most web pages have a dedicated footer section. HTML5 provides the `<footer>` element for this purpose.

Table 2.6 Tag used in this task

Tag	Function
`<footer>...</footer>`	Creates an HTML footer section on a web page or in a `<section>` or `<article>` element.

The `<footer>` element requires both a start and an end tag and any content between the tags will be displayed in the footer section. The `<footer>` element can also be applied to a section or an individual article as well as to a web page. In the instance of an article footer, it might contain a link to the main site where the article is located, a byline for the journalist or writer or links to related articles.

For your information

I've mentioned that elements require a start and an end tag and, based on what you've learned so far in the book about HTML tags and elements, that might seem obvious to the point it doesn't bear stating, but not all HTML elements require both these tags. In some elements – called open elements – the end tag is optional. Older versions of HTML also required a forward slash in open tags (like this: `<br />`), but HTML5 doesn't.

Did you know?

While some web pages list information about article writers in article footers, HTML5 provides an address element (`<address>...</address>`) for this purpose. It's not considered standard-compliant to list author information in the `<footer>` element, but an `<address>` element may be wrapped in a `<footer>` element.

Important

The footer is related to whatever element you add it to. It's a page footer if it's added to the `<body>` element of a page. It's a section footer if it's added before the end tag of a `<section>` element. If added to an `<article>` element it's an article footer and so on.

Creating an HTML footer (cont.)

The results of this task are simple and, like all the others in this chapter, not immediately visible without the assistance of CSS to highlight and format the changes. In this instance, we will create both page and section footers and colour them to stand out for clarity.

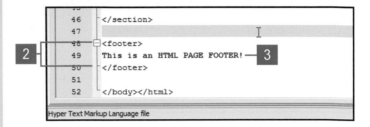

1 Open your sample HTML document in your text editor and save it with a new name.

2 In the `<body>` element, below all the other elements but above the end tag, add an HTML `<footer>` element (that is, type `<footer>` and `</footer>`).

3 Between the tags, type 'This is an HTML PAGE FOOTER!'

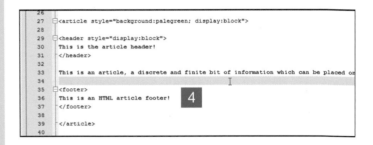

4 In the first `<article>` element on the page, add a `<footer>` element between the tags, under any other text which may be in the element but above the `<article>` end tag.

5 Save the HTML document and open it in your web browser.

6 Locate the footer text you entered on your sample web page. If you need to modify the footers to see them more clearly, add the same inline style to the start tags as you did in the last task.

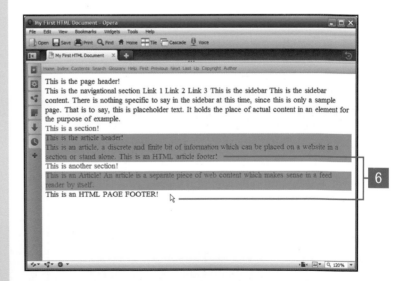

HTML text markup tags

Introduction

The Internet is a collection of pages which are, at least for the moment, still largely made up of text. Because most of the web is text, most of HTML concerns itself with marking up text so it makes sense, is visually pleasing to the viewer and can be understood by web browsers, web designers and programmers alike.

The web is perhaps most analogous to a magazine. There are images, static and video, and words including paragraphs, headings, citations, lists, terms and their definitions and more. Some words are italicised, some are set in bold, and various other formatting is applied to make the items viewed visually interesting and pleasing. HTML can do many of these things with simple tags and elements applied directly to textual content on a web page.

Most of the appearance of a web page is now handled by Cascading Style Sheets (CSS). A great level of control and variation is available to web designers this way, but *general* formatting is still available in HTML and structuring text into organised groups, such as paragraphs and citations, is done with HTML. CSS is used to enhance how those structures look, but their creation relies on HTML.

This chapter allows you to experiment with basic HTML formatting and apply it to parts of your rough web page. You'll see how the paragraph element – `<p>...</p>` – is used to put both text and other elements into a paragraph-style separation from other parts of the web page. There are other ways to do

What you'll do

Learn to break text into paragraphs

Add HTML headings

Format text with HTML

Create an ordered list

Create an unordered list

Create a description list

Use HTML quotations

this (as you learned by applying very simple inline CSS styles to elements in the last chapter), but the paragraph element can be used to simple but effective ends as well.

You'll also explore how to apply headings to pages, sections, articles and other areas of a web page. HTML allows six levels of heading formatting – `<h1>` to `<h6>`. Each represents a heading level on an outline, but each one can be formatted independently using CSS so the same level of heading can appear different on different parts of the page. You will apply heading formatting to header sections you created on your sample web page previously.

HTML can also create ordered lists (`<ol>`...`</ol>`) with numbered items (`<li>`...`</li>`) or unordered lists (`<ul>`...`</ul>`) with bullet points (`<li>`...`</li>`). Definition-style lists – with entries similar to those you might see on a lexicon or dictionary page – are another list type defined by HTML and they include tags for both the defined term (`<dt>`...`</dt>`) and the definition text itself (`<dd>`...`</dd>`). Finally, you'll explore using inline quotation tags for short quotes (`<q>`...`</q>`) and block quote tags (`<blockquote>`...`</blockquote>`) to display larger sections of quoted material. The citation element (`<cite>`...`</cite>`) then lets you refer to cited titles or materials using its own element.

The most basic grouping for text is into paragraphs. With HTML, a paragraph can serve as both a logical block grouping for text, such as in print, or it can separate an element or content from the surrounding content. The HTML paragraph element is therefore one of the most versatile text formatting tools available.

Table 3.1 Tag used in this task

Tag	Function
`<p>...</p>`	Creates an HTML paragraph from text content.

The paragraph element requires a start tag, but the end tag is optional. It is good practice, however, to enclose all paragraph text in the full element – `<p>` *and* `</p>`.

Any text placed in a paragraph element appears as a single paragraph regardless of where line breaks may have been placed in the text editor. Like paragraphs in word processors, HTML paragraphs do not have indented first lines and are, by default, ranged left (or left-aligned).

Jargon buster

Line break – The end of a line of text, either as a result of encountering the page margin or by manual insertion of a line break, such as a carriage return on a manual typewriter or pressing the **Enter** key on a computer keyboard when using word processing software.

Left-aligned – Text is ranged left with a ragged (or unjustified) right margin.

Breaking text into paragraphs

Important

Not placing the end tag at the end of a paragraph element forces the browser to try and figure out where one ends and the next paragraph begins. While using only the start tag is a common practice, it's always safer to use the end tag as well as a good code habit and to ensure proper interpretation of your markup.

3

For your information

Paragraph formatting can be manipulated in numerous ways using CSS. Because CSS is simply more powerful and efficient for shaping the appearance of content, much of the former formatting capabilities of HTML have been deprecated or removed. While they may still function in web browsers, the preferred method is to use CSS.

Breaking text into paragraphs (cont.)

Web browsers also handle text wrapping automatically, so if there is a specific place where the text must move to a new line, it's necessary to use the break tag (`<br>`). Web browsers see this as Microsoft Word or OpenOffice Writer word processing software see the **Enter** key. Without the break tag, the text will wrap at browser-determined margins (unless CSS has been used to establish them, of course).

This exercise is very productive, though simple and straightforward. As you will see in the web browser window, the paragraph element separates its content from other content with white space by creating a 'blank line' between the paragraph element and other content. This provides visual clarity even the simple CSS inline style couldn't achieve with the `display:block` property. That is because the CSS property sets the content in its own block, but doesn't provide the white space.

Paragraph elements can also be used to generate white space free from any content. This is achieved by using an 'empty paragraph' element.

Important

When using an empty paragraph to create white space, it's good practice to include a non-breaking space in the paragraph element. This is done with a special character. Special characters are discussed later in detail, but suffice to say here that a non-breaking space is inserted with the character command ` ` -- the ampersand, nbsp and the ending semicolon are all part of this special character.

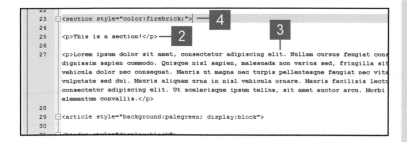

Breaking text into paragraphs (cont.)

Timesaver tip

To get placeholder text used in printing and graphics design known as 'Lorem ipsum' text, visit a lorem ipsum generator (such as at: **http://lipsum.com/**). You can then generate sample text to copy and paste as needed. This was used to generate the 'Lorem ipsum' text used in the screenshot for step 3.

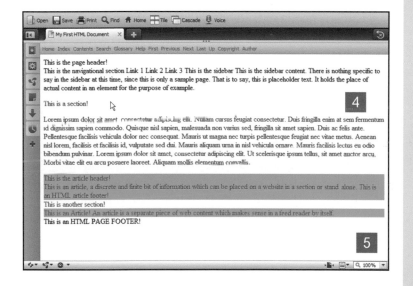

1 Open the sample web page you made in the last chapter in your text editor and save it with a new name.

2 Put the paragraph start tag to the left of the 'This is a section!' placeholder text and then place the end tag at the end of the sentence.

3 In the `<body>` element, in the first section, and before the first `<article>` element, write enough text to make a recognisable paragraph, using the same start and end tags. The standard placeholder 'Lorem ipsum' text has been used here.

4 Remove the `display:block` statement from the inline style of the `<section>` start tag. Be careful *not* to remove the `color:firebrick:` command.

5 Save your HTML file and open it in your web browser.

Adding HTML headings

HTML provides six different headings to use for outlining headings and subheadings. Each is represented by a heading tag followed by a number indicating the heading level. So, `<h1>` represents the top or first level heading, `<h2>` the next level `<h3>` follows and so forth to `<h6>`.

Table 3.2 Tags used in this task

Tag	Function
`<h1>...</h1>`	Specifies a top-level HTML heading.
`<h2>...</h2>`	Specifies a second-level heading.
`<h3>...</h3>`	Specifies a third-level heading.
`<h4>...</h4>`	Specifies a fourth-level heading.
`<h5>...</h5>`	Specifies a fifth-level heading.
`<h6>...</h6>`	Specifies a sixth-level heading.

Headings are used in an HTML document in a similar way to those in any document. They highlight the topics of different print sections, allow readers to scan documents and provide visual 'breaks' for readers' eyes, giving them places to 'rest' as they read.

The `<h1>` element is generally reserved for top-level headings, such as titles. The title of an article or even a section of a website might be labelled using an `<h1>` element. The `<h2>` element, then, is generally a first level of subheading or subtitle, while `<h3>` usually denotes sections within the first-level subheading divisions. Each of those are subsequently broken down by the `<h4>`, `<h5>` and `<h6>` headings.

Think in terms of an outline. The top-most level of an outline is denoted by `<h1>` elements. The next level is `<h2>` and that level is itself subdivided by `<h3>` headings and so on. A new heading at a higher level indicates a new section of the outline, whereas a new heading of a lower rank indicates a subdivision of the current topic. That's what headers do – they organise the page into topics, subjects, divisions and subdivisions which are clearly and easily discernible to the eye.

Heading elements require both a start and an end tag. If you don't use an end tag, all the text which follows the start tag will be interpreted by the browser as part of the heading level and will be modified to display accordingly.

Headings can be grouped together using the `<hgroup>` element. This allows you to 'flatten' the outline so that a title and its subtitle, or a heading and its subheading, are viewed only at the top level in outline format. This only works for outline or summary views of the document, however – the `<hgroup>` element does not have any visual impact on the web page.

This task is very easy to both accomplish and identify on the page. You will add headings to your sample web page and the results will be easy to see. The formatting applied to each heading is easily manipulated using CSS, which will be covered from Chapter 10 onwards.

1 Open your sample web page in your text editor and save it with a new name.

3

Timesaver tip

The **Home** and **End** keys on your keyboard can be used to take you to the beginning or end of a line. Use the **Home** key to move the cursor to the far left, or the beginning, of a line of text or the start of a paragraph (as long as the word wrap feature of your text editor is set to off). Use the **End** key to go to the end of a line or paragraph in a single button click the same way. It moves the cursor to the far right of any text.

Adding HTML headings (cont.)

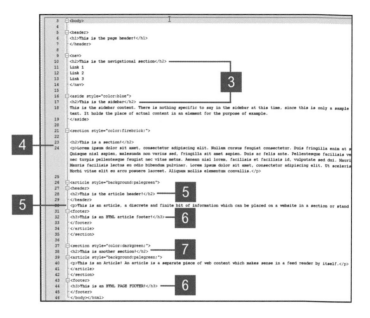

2 In the first `<header>` element, find the text 'This is the page header!' and place an HTML heading 1 element around it: the start tag goes to the left of the text, the end tag at the end of the text.

3 Find the `<nav>` element and add an `<h2>` element to the text 'This is the navigational section'. Do the same for 'This is the sidebar' in the `<aside>` element.

4 Locate the first `<section>` and replace the `<p>` element with an `<h2>` element for the text 'This is a section!'

5 In the first article, wrap the text which says 'This is the article header!' with an `<h2>` element and the paragraph which reads 'This is an article, a discrete and finite bit of …' with a paragraph element. (Be sure to put the end tag at the end of the text, not at the point where it has been cut off here. See the screenshot where the `<p>` is annotated with a number 5 if you're confused.)

Timesaver tip

Use the search and replace feature in your text editor to locate text, tags and properties in your HTML document quickly and easily. Generally, the **F3** key on a keyboard is the **Find Next …** function, which will take you to the next instance of the item you're searching for. If there are no more instances, the search dialogue box will indicate it cannot find the item.

6 Put an `<h3>` element around
the text 'This is an HTML
article footer!' and another
`<h3>` element around the
text 'This is an HTML PAGE
FOOTER!'

7 Find the text 'This is another
section!' and wrap it with an
`<h2>` element, then locate
the text of the second article
element on the page and wrap
it in a paragraph element
(`<p>`...`</p>`).

8 Remove the
`display:block`
properties from all the inline
styles on the page.

9 Save the HTML file and open
it in your web browser.

Important

Don't panic if the formatting you applied via inline
styles doesn't work after you have applied the heading
and paragraph tags described in this task. The browser
interprets the new tags differently from the elements
which have the formatting, so the styles aren't applied
anymore. Do notice, however, how much more
visual clarity the page has, even without the coloured
backgrounds.

Formatting text with HTML

Most of the burden of making text look good on a web page has been taken over by CSS, which, frankly, does a much better job of formatting and adjusting the appearance of text and elements on a page than HTML. HTML still allows text formatting in a few ways, however, so the remaining tags are easy to remember and use.

Before CSS came into its own as the formatting tool of choice for web design, HTML provided basic ways to format text and adjust its appearance on the screen. Some of those ways have survived into HTML5, while others have been deprecated into oblivion and are not supported by modern browsers.

Formatting text is simple in HTML. Just enclose the desired content in the element tags to achieve the effect you want. The different elements provide different ways to display text and some of the more modern elements place the burden of deciding what to display on the browser rather than the code, as with the emphasis (`<em>...</em>`) element or the sample (`<samp>...</samp>`) element.

The limitations of HTML and the cluttering of code resulting from using attributes for formatting have largely been eliminated by the advances in CSS, but it may still be necessary to format text inline from time to time and using HTML tags is fast and easy. Note that while this book offers a sample of the HTML elements available, it is by no means exhaustive, so, to supplement your knowledge, you can find many guides online, such as the HTML5 draft standard letter specifications document from the WHATWG (World Hypertext Application Technology Workgroup, at: **www.whatwg.org/specs/web-apps/current-work/multipage**), or the W3Schools reference (at: **http://w3schools.com**).

The results of this task are clear. For each of the elements you will add, the text will change. Most of the changes may appear identical, such as with the code and sample elements or the emphasis and italic elements. They demonstrate, however, logical versus physical formatting – that is, between cases where the code and italic elements are applied directly to the *text* and where the emphasis and sample elements allow the *browser* to do the work as *it* interprets those elements.

For your information

It may be impossible to distinguish between elements such as the strong element or the bold element when they are applied to content, but HTML differentiates them for a reason. Using formatting elements such as bold and italic (`<b>...</b>` and `<i>...</i>`, respectively) apply formatting *directly* to the text. The strong (`<strong>...</strong>`) and emphasis (`<em>...</em>`) elements, however, allow *the browser* to decide how to display emphasised or strongly emphasised content. It's a subtle but significant difference.

Table 3.3 Tags used in this task

Tag	Function
`<em>...</em>`	Specifies content to be emphasised or stressed.
`<i>...</i>`	Specifies text content which is offset from the rest of the content to signify an alternative mood, voice or other factor. This was formerly the italic element and still italicises text.
`<strong>...</strong>`	Specifies text which has strong importance for the content.
`<b>...</b>`	Specifies content to appear bold.
`<small>...<small>`	Specifies text which is displayed smaller than the surrounding text.
`<sub>...</sub>`	Specifies text to be displayed as subscript.
`<sup>...</sup>`	Specifies text to be displayed as superscript.
`<del>...</del>`	Specifies text to be shown as deleted, with a horizontal line through it. Also known as strikethrough.
`<ins>...</ins>`	Specifies inserted content.
`<var>...</var>`	Specifies the enclosed content as a variable.
`<code>...</code>`	Specifies content as computer code.
`<samp>...</samp>`	Specifies content as sample computer code.
`<cite>...</cite>`	Specifies the name of a cited source, such as an author, book title, journal, article. Not to be confused with the **cite** attribute of the HTML **<quote>** and **<blockquote>** elements.
` `	Specifies a line break in content.

Formatting text with HTML (cont.)

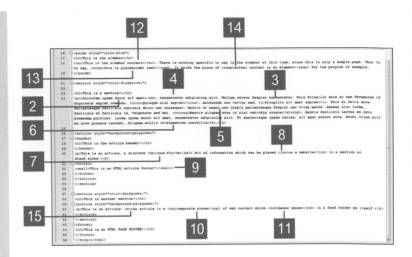

1 Open your sample web page in your text editor and save it with a new name.

2 Find the 'Lorem ipsum' paragraph you inserted in the first `<section>` in the last task and put an emphasis element (`<em>...</em>`) around the words 'Lorem ipsum dolor sit amet'.

3 Locate the words 'fringilla sit amet sapien' and enclose them in the italic (`<i>...</i>`) element.

4 Find the words 'Quisque nisl sapien' and enclose them in a cite element (`<cite>...</cite>`).

5 Find the words 'Mauris aliquam urna in nisl vehicula ornare' and enclose them with the strong (`<strong>...</strong>`) element.

6 Enclose the words 'elementum convallis' at the end of the 'Lorem ipsum' paragraph with the bold (`<b>...</b>`) element.

7 Find the first article, and locate the words 'and finite' in the content. Enclose them with a delete (`<del>...</del>`) element.

Important

Like all inline formatting elements, the `<em>` element requires both a start and an end tag. Leaving the end tag off will result in all text after the start tag being emphasis formatted.

For your information

The `<h3>` element could have been left in place and the `<small>` element added to it, formatting the element with both. Having elements inside other elements in this way is called nesting elements. You have been asked to remove the heading in this task to make the results more obvious when you view the page in your browser.

Jargon buster

Superscript – Text which is elevated above the line of text slightly and reduced in size. Superscript numbers are often used to indicate footnotes and in mathematics, measurements and so on to indicate a number is squared or to the power of, such as $2m^2$.

Subscript – Text which is lowered beneath the line of text slightly and reduced in size. Subscript text is used in notation for chemicals, such as H_2O.

For your information

The variable element doesn't declare a variable as it would in a programming language. Rather, it simply acts as a placeholder for prose or can be used to represent an actual variable in mathematics or a programming language.

8 Find the words 'on a website' in this sentence and enclose it with an insert (`<ins>`... `</ins>`) element.

9 Find the article footer and replace the `<h3>`... `</h3>` element with the small (`<small>`... `</small>`) element. Remember to replace both the start and end tags.

10 In the second article, place a superscript (`<sup>`... `</sup>`) element around the words 'separate piece'.

11 Place a subscript (`<sub>`...`</sub>`) element around the words 'makes sense' later in the same sentence.

12 Enclose the words 'This is the sidebar content' in the aside element in a variable (`<var>`...`</var>`) element.

13 Wrap the words 'this is placeholder text' in the `<code>`...`</code>` element.

14 Use a `<samp>`...`</samp>` element to enclose the words 'actual content in an element'.

3

Formatting text with HTML (cont.)

15 Find the second `<article>` again. Insert a `<br>` tag in front of the sentence which begins with the words 'An article…'.

16 Save the HTML file and open it in your web browser.

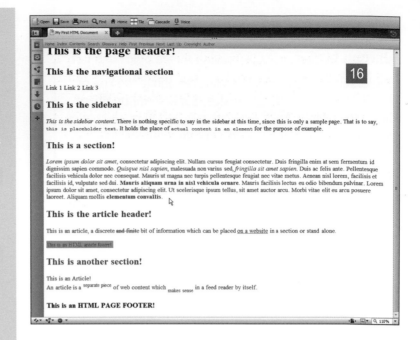

White space is an important factor for readability in both print and online pages. As time becomes more and more valuable and less and less available, making things quick and easy to read becomes ever more critical. Most people simply don't have time to plod through reams of text, either online or in print. Wise use of white space helps with that issue. Lists also are an important and valuable tool for web page design.

Lists are generally short, numbered or have bullet points and provide bite-sized portions of text to scan. HTML offers several types of lists, but the two primary types are numbered lists and bulleted lists. Numbered lists are called ordered lists, while bulleted or unnumbered lists are called unordered lists.

Table 3.4 Tags used in this task

Tag	Function
`<ol>...</ol>`	Creates an ordered list, with numbered list items.
`<li>...</li>`	Creates an item in an ordered or unordered list.

Ordered lists are typically used where the order of the items in the list is important. Once specified by the ordered list element (`<ol>...</ol>`), ordered lists automatically number their list items sequentially from the top to the bottom of the list or from left to right if they are not separated by a line break in the HTML file. In the browser window, they will always display from top to bottom with numbers ascending in value to the end.

For your information

It is possible to use attributes to alter the start number of an ordered list or specify whether the list numbers are ascending (1, 2, 3 …) or descending (3, 2, 1 …). CSS is the preferred method for formatting lists in other ways, however.

Creating an ordered list (cont.)

1 Open your sample web page in your text editor and save it with a new name.

2 Find the navigation (`<nav>`) element and remove any manual line breaks you added so that the text is all on one line, separated only by spaces.

3 Wrap the contents of the `<nav>` element in an ordered list element (`<ol>...</ol>`), leaving out the text 'This is the navigational section'.

4 Wrap the text 'Link 1' with a list item element (`<li>...</li>`).

5 Do the same for the 'Link 2' and 'Link 3' content. Create additional link placeholders if you like, wrapping each with the list item element.

So, for instance, a list in text form would be something like this:

> For my omelette, I'm going to use (1) eggs, (2) cheese, (3) mushrooms, (4) onions, (5) tomatoes, (6) peppers and (7) ham.

A simple, seven-item list, but it looks much longer laid out this way and isn't easy to follow. The same list in an ordered list format, however, is much better:

> For my omelette, I'm going to use:
> 1. Eggs
> 2. Cheese
> 3. Mushrooms
> 4. Onions
> 5. Tomatoes
> 6. Peppers
> 7. Ham

While it extends further down the page vertically, the eye can move over the list and take in the content quickly and easily.

The results of this task are readily visible. You will take some of the content of your web page and make it into an ordered list, providing more white space and giving the eye something to scan as it looks over the page without compromising the information contained.

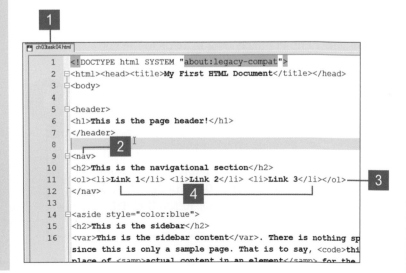

Important

Be sure to keep your ordered list element end tag *inside* the end tag for the navigational element!

For your information

It is actually more common for navigational links to be formatted as unordered lists than ordered lists as we've done here. This has been done here only for the purpose of demonstration, but it is not normal practice.

6 Save the HTML file and open it in your web browser.

3

Creating an unordered list

Unordered lists are very similar to ordered lists in behaviour and attributes, but are typically used when the order in which items are listed isn't important. They are bulleted lists. The attributes allow you to specify what types of bullet points you want to use, but, again, this formatting is best left to CSS rather than HTML. HTML provides the structure for them, though.

Bulleted lists make for terrific navigational or sidebar link formatting. They also make long articles or text pieces seem less daunting and offer the same benefits of white space as ordered lists, with the added benefit of the items having no particular order. Bulleted or unordered lists are also commonly used in navigational sections of web pages to create links in an orderly, organised fashion without numbering.

Table 3.5 Tags used in this task

Tag	Function
`<ul>...</ul>`	Creates an HTML unordered list, where the items are not numbered but bulleted.
`<li>...</li>`	Creates an item in an ordered or unordered list.

In this task, you will create an unordered list in the `<aside>` element to organise your sample web page. The results are simple and immediately visible. As you will see from your work, the sidebar will be much more visually appealing and easier to understand. This is one of many uses for unordered lists.

Important

The `<ul>...</ul>` element requires both a start and an end tag, as do most structural elements. It does not, however, always require any list item elements (`<li>`) within it.

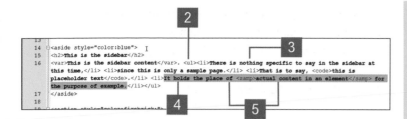

1 Open your sample web page in your text editor and save it with a new name.

2 In the `<aside>` element, place all the content after the `<var>` element in an unordered list element.

3 Put the text 'There is nothing specific to say in the sidebar at this time' into a list item element.

4 Place the text 'since this is only a sample page' into another list item element.

5 Repeat this process for the statements 'That is to say, `<code>` this is placeholder text `</code>`' and 'It holds the place of `<samp>`actual content in an element `</samp>` for the purpose of example.'

6 Save the HTML file and open it in your web browser.

Important

!

The list item element does not require an end tag and allows nesting items to create an outline-style list. Be sure to close each list item with an end tag for this exercise, though, to avoid confusion about where each list item is. In practice, it is at the discretion of the web designer whether to add this or not.

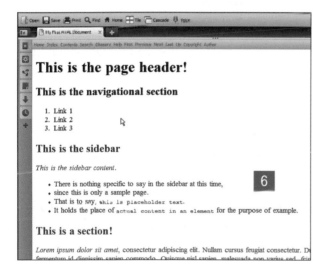

For your information

i

Unordered lists can be used to great effect in conjunction with other structural elements (such as `<aside>`, `<section>` or `<footer>` elements) to create site maps and multilevel navigational aids for a website.

Creating a description list

Another possible list type using HTML is the description list. Think of this as a glossary or dictionary-style list, where a term is set apart as the term to be described and the list items beneath it represent the descriptions for that glossary or dictionary entry, a bit like this:

Defined term
> Description one for the term
> Description two for the term
> Description three for the term

Note the descriptions are indented from the description term slightly – that is, the description term is formatted with a hanging indent from the definitions.

Each description list needs at least one name, or term, to be described and any number of descriptions or definitions. Each description list requires both start and end tags and must contain at least one definition term element and at least one description element for the term.

Table 3.6 Tags used in this task

Tag	Function
`<dl>...</dl>`	Creates a description list, a definition-style list.
`<dt>...</dt>`	Specifies a description term or definition term.
`<dd>...</dd>`	Specifies a definition, description or value for a term or name in a description list.

A description list is created using the description list element (`<dl>...</dl>`). The term to be described or defined is specified using the definition term tag or element (`<dt>...</dt>`), while the definition for the term is specified using the description tag or element (`<dd>...</dd>`).

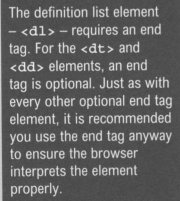

Important

!

The definition list element – `<dl>` – requires an end tag. For the `<dt>` and `<dd>` elements, an end tag is optional. Just as with every other optional end tag element, it is recommended you use the end tag anyway to ensure the browser interprets the element properly.

Description lists are very useful when putting together glossaries, defining jargon or unusual terms, and for such things as FAQ pages or sections. They're also very useful for lists of instructions in certain cases where an ordered or unordered list would not be a good choice.

The results of this task are clear. You will add some text to your sample web page and place it in description lists, then apply some formatting to the list with the heading elements you learned about earlier in this chapter. The definition list should be obvious in the browser window.

1 Open your sample web page in the text editor and save it with a new name.

2 Find the 'Lorem ipsum' paragraph in your document and select and copy all the text.

3 Add a few blank lines below the 'Lorem ipsum' paragraph and paste the copied text and all markup elements in the new space.

3

Creating a description list (cont.)

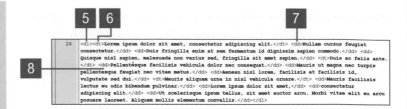

4 Remove all the elements from the new paragraph, including the paragraph elements (`<p>`...`</p>`).

5 Enclose the paragraph in a description list element (`<dl>`...`</dl>`).

6 Make the first sentence the definition term by wrapping it in a `<dt>` element.

7 Make the next three sentences descriptions or definitions by wrapping them with `<dd>` elements.

8 Make the fifth sentence another description term (`<dt>`) and make the remaining sentences all definitions (`<dd>`). Put the last two sentences into a single definition element if you like.

9 Save the HTML file and open it in your browser.

Timesaver tip

Using the copy and paste feature of your text editor can help you with repetitive text mark up such as is required in this task. Just copy the start tag and paste it to the beginning and end of the content, changing the end tags by adding the terminating forward slash (`</>`).

When quoting the work of others in print, you must attribute the sources of those quotes. The same is true for web pages.

HTML has two methods for quoting others in your content. They are the quote (`<q>...</q>`) and the block quote (`<blockquote>...</blockquote>`) elements.

Table 3.7 Tags used in this task

Tags	Function
`<q>...</q>`	Specifies a short, inline quote in HTML. Used with the `cite` attribute to link the quote to its source address, if available.
`<blockquote>... </blockquote>`	Specifies a longer section quoted from another source in HTML to appear as a block, indented. Used with the `cite` attribute to link the quote to its source address, if available.

The quote element specifies a short quotation from another source, such as a sentence or two, or any quotation which might be used in line with the rest of your content. In other words, quotes which aren't long enough to require separation from other content. The element requires both a start and an end tag to denote where the quotation starts and stops and is usually used with the `cite` attribute to specify the address of the source you quoted.

The block quote element specifies a longer quotation, which needs to be set apart from the rest of the content due to length or importance of the material. A block quote element requires both a start and an end tag and, like the quotation element, uses the `cite` attribute to link the quote to its source address. The block quote element separates the quote from the rest of the content with white space.

Jargon buster

Attribute – A specific property of an HTML element which alters how it is displayed or how it behaves. HTML element attributes are included in the start tag of the element.

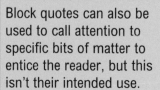

For your information

Block quotes can also be used to call attention to specific bits of matter to entice the reader, but this isn't their intended use.

3

Using HTML quotations (cont.)

1. Open the sample web page in the text editor and save it with a new name.

2. Copy the 'Lorem ipsum' placeholder text and paste it to form a new paragraph in the first `<article>` element, beneath the existing paragraph.

3. Locate the sentence beginning 'Pellentesque facilisis vehicular …' and place the start tag for a block quote element in front of it (`<blockquote>`).

4. Place the end tag for the block quote element (`</blockquote>`) after the word 'pulvinar' a few sentences later.

Important

Don't confuse the `cite` *attribute* of a quotation element with the cite *element*, which is covered in the next task. The `cite` attribute is strictly used within the HTML quotation elements to link the quote to its source address.

This task is very straightforward and the results are visually obvious. You will be using the block quote element in the first `<article>` element to separate it from the rest of the sentence and display it with white space above and below it and indent it a bit. In the second `<article>` element, the result is quotation marks will be inserted around the sentence portion which you will enclose with the quote element. Neither of the examples uses the `<cite>` element to reference the source address in this case, of course, as it is not a real web page but that is the normal practice with both elements.

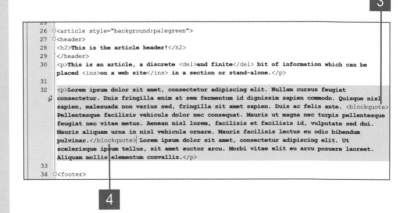

```
25
26  <article style="background:palegreen">
27  <header>
28  <h2>This is the article header!</h2>
29  </header>
30  <p>This is an article, a discrete <del>and finite</del> bit of information which can be
    placed <ins>on a web site</ins> in a section or stand-alone.</p>
31
32  <p>Lorem ipsum dolor sit amet, consectetur adipiscing elit. Nullam cursus feugiat
    consectetur. Duis fringilla enim at sem fermentum id dignissim sapien commodo. Quisque nisl
    sapien, malesuada non varius sed, fringilla sit amet sapien. Duis ac felis ante. <blockquote>
    Pellentesque facilisis vehicula dolor nec consequat. Mauris ut magna nec turpis pellentesque
    feugiat nec vitae metus. Aenean nisl lorem, facilisis et facilisis id, vulputate sed dui.
    Mauris aliquam urna in nisl vehicula ornare. Mauris facilisis lectus eu odio bibendum
    pulvinar.</blockquote> Lorem ipsum dolor sit amet, consectetur adipiscing elit. Ut
    scelerisque ipsum tellus, sit amet auctor arcu. Morbi vitae elit eu arcu posuere laoreet.
    Aliquam mollis elementum convallis.</p>
33
34  <footer>
```

```
40  <section style="color:darkgreen;">
41  <h2>This is another section!</h2>
42  <article style="background:palegreen;">
43  <p>This is an Article! <br>An article is <q>a separate piece of web content which makes sense in a
    feed reader by itself</q>.</p>
44  </article>
```

6

7

5 Locate the second `<article>` element on the page and remove all the markup except for any paragraph elements and break tags.

6 Find the sentence beginning 'An article is a separate piece …' and wrap it in a quote element (`<q>`… `</q>`), starting from the word 'a'. Place the end tag before the full stop at the end of the sentence.

7 Save the HTML file and open it in your web browser.

3

HTML hyperlinks

Introduction

Imagine you're grocery shopping. The shop's fruit and vegetable section is far from the dairy section and that's across the shop from the bakery, which is equally far from the deli. You need things from each of those sections, so you're in for a lot of walking. You have a laptop, though, and your shopping list is on it in a set of hyperlinks. By clicking the items on your list, they are transported from their locations in the shop to you. A few clicks and you've finished shopping.

That's how hyperlinks on a web page work. They contain information which allows your browser to fetch the resource listed – whether it's another page on the same site, a new site or some multimedia item from another source – and bring it to your screen for you.

Your browser doesn't see the video, audio file or the image you see when it reads a hyperlink. All it sees is text, and nothing else. A hyperlink sends the browser to the correct resource to put it on to your page or asks it to replace the current resource with the requested one.

What you'll do

Come to understand URLs

Use absolute URLs

Use relative URLs

Create hyperlink anchors

Add hyperlink targets

Create a hyperlink to an e-mail address

The hyperlink itself is a set of instructions to make those resource requests. They contain specific addresses to locate the documents, videos, audio files, text and images from all over the world. Hyperlinks allow you to hop from item to item and view the resources at those specific addresses, wherever they are in the world.

Those addresses are called Uniform Resource Locators (URLs). Every web page in the world, any resource on the web, whether it's pure text or a mixture of text and multimedia or graphics, has its own specific URL. It is these URLs which are the key to hyperlinks.

Uniform Resource Locators (URLs) are the long lines of characters you see in the address bar of your web browser whenever you visit resources or pages. They are made up of several elements, such as the protocol used to transport the data, the web server's address as a domain name, the specific location on the web server and the specific name of the resource itself. All of this makes up the URL of any site, document, file or resource of any kind on the Internet.

Think of the URL as an address. It contains the town, street and specific house number, but it can also specify a location within the house itself and sometimes even a particular place in a particular room. So a URL is like a postal address, but a very, very specific address.

http://www.webserver.com/path/resource/

| Protocol | Web server's name | Path to resource | Resource name |

The Hypertext Transport Protocol (HTTP) is the primary set of data packet headers used to move data across the Internet. The first part of the URL shows the protocol – HTTP – which lets the computers involved know they are exchanging a web page. Everything after the colon in the URL represents the URL of the resource being requested.

After the protocol is the web server's name. It is also known as the domain name. It is the Internet computer the requested resource is stored on.

After the web server's name is the path. This is similar to the path taken to access documents on a Windows computer or a Mac computer. You save items in a folder or directory or in a subfolder in the directory. The path is made up of the directories and subdirectories which hold the resource.

The final part of the URL is the resource name itself, whether it's a web page, video, an audio file or image.

4

Understanding
URLs (cont.)

To return to our image above of a URL being like a postal address, then the URL indicates the city, street and house number, the room and sometimes the part of the room in which the resource is stored. Something like:

Flat 3, Black Oak House, 123 Anystreet, Anytown

It goes further, though. The URL then indicates:

master bedroom, computer desk, second filing drawer, third folder

Some of the paths for resources on web servers can be quite long, as a result.

In this exercise, you will explore some URLs for large Internet-based companies and examine the paths and resource names in their addresses. You will also look at how different resource requests change the URL as the resource comes up.

1. Open your web browser and type '**uk.yahoo.com**' in the address bar, then press **Enter**.

2. When the Yahoo! page loads, notice the URL. The browser adds '**http://**' to the URL for you, but does not add the '**www**' portion.

3. Click on the Lifestyle link on the sidebar on the left. When the page loads, notice the URL shifts to **http://uk.lifestyle. yahoo.com**.

4. Click other links on the sidebar and watch the URL shift for each one.

For your information

The examples in this task are from Yahoo!, but similar experiments could be conducted with most websites. Notice that the base URL, which is made up of the protocol (**http:**), and the domain name (**//uk.yahoo.com/**) do not change as you explore other articles online. Only the resources change from request to request (**main_page**, **url** and so on). The resource name is the last part of the URL. Different companies might handle the URLs differently, but this example and so on shows how the mechanisms work.

4

Using absolute URLs

If you think of URLs as specific locations in a specific place, absolute URLs contain the full address – the country, city, street, block of flats, flat, room, location in the room. To move to a new house or block of flats, a new URL is needed to make the move happen. Absolute URLs provide all the information to make such a move and always include all the information.

In the case of an absolute URL, the information is actually the protocol, domain name, path and resource. All of those pieces of information are required for an absolute URL to link to a location.

Absolute URLs are most often used to link websites. While you can use absolute URLs to link sections of the same document or different documents on the same site, they are best suited to *new* locations on the Internet, where the entire URL is required.

For your information

Linking to portions of the same document or to other documents on the same website is best done using relative URLs, which are discussed in the next task.

Referencing other URLs or locations is done using the anchor tag (`<a>...</a>`). The anchor tag can reference other sections of the same page, a different page on the same site or a new site altogether. The location is specified in an attribute of the anchor tag, called the `href` attribute (`href` stands for hyperlink reference). So, linking to Yahoo!'s website requires an anchor tag such as this:

```
<a href="http://uk.yahoo.com/">
Yahoo! UK</a>.
```

This markup will turn the 'Yahoo! UK' text into a hyperlink to Yahoo! UK's website. Clicking it with the mouse will cause the web browser to bring Yahoo!'s homepage to your screen.

Table 4.1 Tag used in this task

Tag	Function
`<a>...</a>`	Specifies an anchor on a web page. The anchor links to a document or other resource on the same page, in a new document on the same site or on a new site. The **href** attribute is required to specify the destination.

Note the features of the **href** attribute. The attribute name (**href**) is followed by an equals sign (`=`), then a set of double quotes (`"`). The absolute URL then follows, including the protocol and domain name. To link to a specific resource on the destination server, the resource must be named as well.

For your information

Remember, a resource can be anything – a web page, video clip, an audio file, image or a graphic, whatever. 'Resource' is used to refer generically to anything the web browser can show you from a web server.

To specify another document on the same site, the resource name must also be listed in the **href** attribute.

In this task, you will link your sample web page to a few of your favourite websites. By clicking on the hyperlinks created using the anchor element (`<a>...</a>`), your browser will open those links in your browser window.

4

Using absolute URLs (cont.)

```
14  ⊟<aside style="color:blue">
15  ⊿<h2>This is the sidebar</h2>
16   <var>This is the sidebar content</var>. <ul><li><a href=
     "http://www.Google.com/">Google Search Engine</a></li> <li><a href=
     "http://uk.yahoo.com">Yahoo!</a></li> <li><a href=
     "http://www.amazon.co.uk">Amazon.com</a></li> <li><a href=
     "www.wikipedia.org">Wikipedia</a></li></ul>
17   </aside>
```

1. Open your sample web page in your text editor and save it with a new name.

2. Find the `<aside>` element within the `<body>` element.

3. In the list's first item element, add a link to a favourite website with the anchor element (`<a href="http://url/path/resource">anchor text</a>`).

4. Change the list item text to the name of the website you have hyperlinked to – Google in our example.

5. Repeat this process for all the list items in the aside element. Make sure you include the double quotes and the full path to the resource you're connecting to, if it's not the site's main page, in each case.

6. Save the HTML file and open it in your web browser. Click each hyperlink and make sure it takes you to the page or resource you hyperlinked to.

Important

The anchor text shown above, except for the URL and path, is the exact format you should use when creating the hyperlinks for this task. If you like, you can copy and paste the anchor tag from one list item element to the next and change the URLs as necessary.

Important

Be sure to leave the `<li>` and `</li>` tags in place, putting the anchor element tags inside the list item element tags, like this: `<li><a href="webpageURL">Web page name</a></li>`.

If we think about the absolute URL as directions to a specific spot in a building, which includes everything from the city down to the exact location in a room, then it's easy to see how this becomes impractical for moving within the *same* room, flat or even block of flats. For example, if I give the directions:

127 Mirror Pond Road, Mirror Pond Court, Flat 5, living room, far left corner

then I don't want to repeat all that information to give instructions to a new location within that same room, flat or even block of flats, such as:

127 Mirror Pond Road, Mirror Pond Court, Flat 5, living room, near right corner

As you can see, this will become cumbersome very quickly. A far faster way would be to include only the necessary information, like this:

living room, bookcase near the window

Then, I don't have to bother to provide all the information which hasn't changed – the street number, the name of the block of flats, flat number, even the room. Only the location *within* the room has changed, which is all that is given.

Instructing the browser where to find a resource with this sort of shorthand uses *relative* URLs instead of *absolute* URLs. Only the relevant information is given, and the location is *relative* to the current resource's location, hence the name.

Relative URLs are the mechanism for hyperlinking different sections of the same document and even different documents on the same site. It allows simpler navigation on a specific site. Moving within the same site only requires the directory name, not the web server's name, as well as the path to the specific resource to create a hyperlink. Tell the browser to look in the directory above or below, in the same directory but a different folder or, if the resource is stored on the same

Using relative URLs

4

Using relative URLs (cont.)

directory, in the same folder, just name the resource. All this is done within the `href` attribute of the anchor element – the browser does the rest.

! Important

It is critical to note that, while the domain name or server name of a web server is never case-sensitive, sometimes the path to a specific resource *is*. It all depends on the operating system used by the web server. If it's a Windows system, then the path is *not* case-sensitive, but, if the web server is a Unix server, it *will* be case-sensitive.

---

i For your information

Navigating directories, folders and subfolders using the anchor element is easy and simple, but does require a bit of knowledge about Unix system navigation or navigating folders in Windows with the command window. Use the command `cd..` to move *up* in the directory structure (the letters 'cd' stand for 'change directory'). Use the command `cd./` to move *down* in the directory structure.

In this task, you will change the `<nav>` element content from an ordered list to an unordered list and create hyperlinks from the list items to other parts of your sample web page. You will then test the links by clicking each one. This should bring you to the section of the document you linked to. You will also find that the **Back** button on your browser should take you back to the `<nav>` element.

For your information

It is a common practice for websites to have their main pages named 'default.htm' or 'index.htm' (or to use the extension 'html'). This ensures that the web server will send the main page to the browser unless the visitor specifies otherwise.

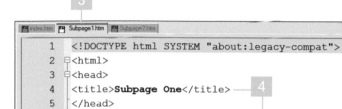

3

```
       Index.htm    Subpage1.htm    Subpage2.htm

 1    <!DOCTYPE html SYSTEM "about:legacy-compat">
 2    <html>
 3    <head>
 4    <title>Subpage One</title>              4
 5    </head>
 6    <body>
 7    <h1>This is Subpage One</h1>
 8
 9    <h2><a href="Index.htm">Home Page</a></h2>
10    </body>
11    </html>
```

1 Create a folder on your computer with the name 'Main Folder' and, inside it, create another folder called 'Subfolder'.

2 Open your sample web page in your text editor, change the title element to 'Home Page' and save it in your Main Folder with the name 'Index.htm'.

3 Open your HTML template from Chapter 1 in your text editor and save it in your Main Folder with the name 'Subpage1.htm'.

4 Change the title element to 'Subpage One'. In the **<body>** element, create an **<h1>** heading with the text 'This is Subpage One', then create an **<h2>** element around the anchor element **<a href="Index. htm">Home Page</a>**.

5 Save Subpage1.htm and close it.

4

Using relative URLs (cont.)

6 Open your HTML template from Chapter 1 in your text editor and save it in your Subfolder with the name 'Subpage2.htm'.

7 Change the `<title>` element to 'Subpage 2'. In the `<body>` element, create an `<h1>` heading with the text 'This is Subpage Two', then create this anchor element: `<a href="../Index.htm">Home Page</a>`, then enclose it in an `<h2>` heading.

8 Save Subpage2.htm and close it.

9 In your sample web page, locate the `<nav>` element and change Link 1 to a hyperlink by wrapping it with this anchor element: `<a href="Subpage1.htm">Link 1</a>`.

10 Change Link 2 to a hyperlink by wrapping it with this anchor element: `<a href="./Subfolder/Subpage2.htm">Link 2</a>`.

Important

Note carefully the command strings used! Every full stop and forward slash and quote mark is an essential part of the hyperlink. It will not work if they are not typed in correctly.

11. Save the Index.htm file and open it in your web browser. Click each link in the 'This is the navigational section' area of the web page.

12. Click the Home Page link on each subpage to return to Index.htm in Main Folder.

4

Creating hyperlink anchors

In the previous two tasks, you have learned to link to external websites and other documents on the same site. Now, you will hyperlink to different parts of the same document.

Connecting different parts of the same document is done via the anchor element and its `href` attribute again. Unlike the other links, however, hyperlinks which connect parts of the *same* document require destinations and for you to reference them by name.

Let's go back to our address analogy. In this instance, rather than specify a new flat in the block or a new room in the flat, you simply specify a new location in the same spot in the same room. If the original location was:

> Elm Glen Towers, 123 High Street, Flat 23, bedroom, desk, second drawer

then your new location can be specified as simply:

> third drawer

and nothing more is required. With hyperlinks, we tell the anchor element where on the page we want to jump to and the browser can locate the new spot and take the screen there.

To hyperlink to other areas of the same document, anchors must be created. In this context, 'anchor' differs from the anchor element, which refers to the instruction set which changes content to a hyperlink. An anchor is a specific type of anchor element which refers to another spot on the same document. For instance, a long document might have a table of contents which is a series of hyperlinks. The hyperlinks in the table of contents take the reader to the different sections listed.

Jargon buster

Anchor – A special hyperlink which contains an `href` element specifying another section of the same document.

Anchors can also link to other anchors on different pages. In this way, a link from one page can go to not just another page but also a specific *section* of another page.

To create the anchor (hyperlink), the `href` attribute must point to another anchor with a `name` attribute instead of an `href` attribute. The name is enclosed in double quotes and preceded by the hash (#) or pound symbol:

```
<a href="#anchor name">Hyperlink Text</a>
```

The hyperlink will take the screen to the anchor location the `name` attribute refers to when clicked. The `name` attribute on the destination anchor does not require the hash symbol:

```
<a name="anchor name">Destination Text</a>
```

In this task you will add anchors to sections of your sample web page and create hyperlinks in the `<nav>` element. You will then test your anchors and verify their function. The results should be straightforward.

1 Open the sample web page you created in your Main Folder for the last task and save it with a new name.

2 Locate the `<nav>` element and add an anchor element within the list item element around Link 3. Set the `href` attribute to 'article' (`<a href="#article">`). Change the text from 'Link 3' to 'First Article'.

3 Add another list item to the unordered list and, within the list item element, add an anchor element with the `href` attribute set to 'article2'. Set the content to 'Second Article'.

4 Locate the first `<article>` in the `<body>` element. Find the `<header>` and add an anchor element within the `<h2>` element. In the start tag, include the `<name>` attribute, and set it to 'article'. Don't forget the end tag.

5 Locate the second `<article>` on the page. In the heading element, add an anchor tag with the name attribute set to 'article2'.

Creating hyperlink anchors (cont.)

6 Save the HTML file and open it in your web browser. Click each of the `<nav>` element links to be taken to different parts of the page.

Now that you know how to create hyperlinks, it might be beneficial to know how to open them where you want them opened. In the old days of the Internet (the 1990s) a lot of pages used frames. Frames divided pages into sections and each frame could have different content. Hyperlinks could open their destinations in a specific frame.

Now, though, frames are a thing of the past. They've been deprecated so long there's no need to learn about them. What lingers from their era, however, is the `target` attribute of the anchor element, which originally specified in which frame the resource would open. Now, instead of specifying the frame, it specifies what the WHATWG calls 'the browsing context'.

The `target` attribute has four valid settings, each of which must be preceded by an underscore (_) and then the target name. The valid settings are `_blank`, `_parent`, `_top` and `_self`.

The setting `_blank` opens the resource in a new window or, if a tabbed interface is used and properly configured, in a new tab. The `_parent` setting opens the resource in the parent browsing context (window or tab) unless there isn't one, in which case it opens the resource in the current context. The `_top` setting opens the resource in the top-most browsing context or in the current context if there isn't a top-most context. The `_self` setting is … well, self-explanatory.

In this task, you will add targets to the external website hyperlinks in the `<aside>` element on your sample web page. Clicking on each one should open the requested site in a new window or, if possible, a new tab in your browser (such as with Opera™, Firefox and later versions of Internet Explorer).

Adding hyperlink targets

4

Adding hyperlink targets (cont.)

1 Open your sample web page in your Main Folder and save it with a new name.

2 Locate the **<nav>** element and, in the anchor elements of the first list item, add the attribute **target="_blank"**.

3 In the second list item anchor element, add the attribute **target="_top"**.

4 In the third list item add the attribute **target="_parent"** to the anchor element.

5 In the fourth list item, add the attribute **target="_self"** to the anchor element.

6 Save the HTML file and open it in your web browser. Test each link and observe the behaviour of the hyperlinks and where they open their destinations.

For your information

For the most part, the only one of these settings you'll use is the **_blank** one. As a web designer, the goal is to retain and attract visitors, not send them away. The **_blank** setting opens the resource requested in a new browser instance or a new tab, depending on browser type and configuration.

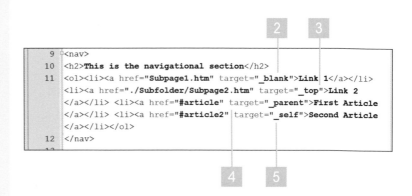

```
 9  <nav>
10  <h2>This is the navigational section</h2>
11  <ol><li><a href="Subpage1.htm" target="_blank">Link 1</a></li>
    <li><a href="./Subfolder/Subpage2.htm" target="_top">Link 2
    </a></li> <li><a href="#article" target="_parent">First Article
    </a></li> <li><a href="#article2" target="_self">Second Article
    </a></li></ol>
12  </nav>
```

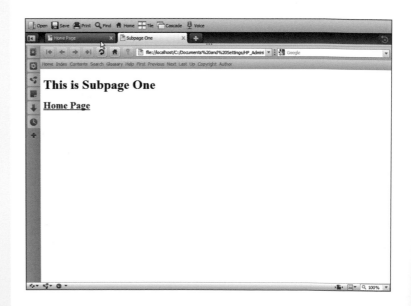

Most websites have a 'Contact us' link somewhere, whether 'us' means 'me' for private sites or 'Customer service' for commercial sites. On many sites, clicking the 'Contact' link opens up a form which you can use to send a message to the intended party. On some sites, however, clicking the 'Contact' link opens your default e-mail program with a header ready for you to enter your message to send to the recipient. These are hyperlinks, nothing more; the only difference between them and the hyperlinks which we've added before is the protocol listed in the **href** attribute of the anchor tag.

Rather than using HTTP as the protocol, linking to an e-mail address uses the **mailto** protocol. In the **href** listing for the destination, the **mailto** protocol and the e-mail address are provided and the hyperlink will open an e-mail message to send to the e-mail address provided.

```
<a href="mailto:recipient@webemail.
com">Contact Me!</a>
```

It's also possible to populate some of the message fields, such as the CC and BCC recipients and subject line. In fact, you can even populate the body of the message if you like. It quickly becomes very cumbersome to populate long messages, though, as you'll see.

To add a subject to the message, place a question mark at the end of the e-mail address, followed by 'subject', then an equals sign (=). Then, type the subject of the message and use **&20** for spaces between words. To insert a CC recipient for the message, add **&cc** to the attribute, then an equals sign (=), followed by the additional e-mail address. Do the same to add a BCC recipient (replacing the CC with BCC, of course). Put body text in using **&body**, then an equals sign and the body of the message, again with **&20** for spaces between words.

```
<a href="mailto:recipient1@webemail.com?
subject=Email&20Subject&20
&cc=recipient2@webemail.com
&bcc=recipient3@webemail.com
&body=I&20am&20contacting&20you."
>Contact us!</a>
```

Creating a hyperlink to an e-mail address

1. Open your sample web page in your Main Folder and save it with a new name.

2. Locate the `<footer>` element with the `<h3>` heading 'This is an HTML PAGE FOOTER!' and change the text to 'Contact me!' and change the `<h3>` heading to an `<h4>` heading.

3. Inside the `<h4>` element, add an anchor element with your actual e-mail address in the `href` attribute (`<a href="mailto:myemail@emailsvc.com">`).

4. Add a CC recipient to a second e-mail address (try to ensure it's an actual e-mail address, though – if you only have one, disregard this and the next step unless someone you know doesn't mind receiving strange e-mails from you).

5. Add a bcc recipient to the `href` attribute.

6. Add the subject 'Testing Hyperlinks' to the `href` attribute.

7. Add the text 'This is a test' to the body of the message.

That's quite a bit of typing, and it's not exactly easy to read, either. Clarity has been added to this example by moving each element of the message to its own lines, but, regardless of this clarity, the enormous amount of typing makes populating more than the subject of the message and very short message bodies impractical.

Important

Note that the entire `href` attribute value is wrapped in double quotes, but none of the individual values within it are wrapped in either single or double quotes. That is because doing so will cause the `href` value to be invalid and the hyperlink will not work.

For your information

Additional e-mail addresses are added by separating them with semicolons. There isn't a limit to how many addresses you can add to each field.

In this task, you will create a hyperlink in the footer of your sample web page which will open up the default e-mail program on a computer and populate the message with a recipient and subject. A brief message will appear in the body of the e-mail as well.

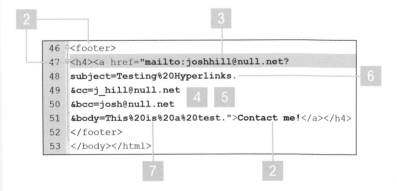

```
46 <footer>
47 <h4><a href="mailto:joshhill@null.net?
48 subject=Testing%20Hyperlinks.
49 &cc=j_hill@null.net
50 &bcc=josh@null.net
51 &body=This%20is%20a%20test.">Contact me!</a></h4>
52 </footer>
53 </body></html>
```

78

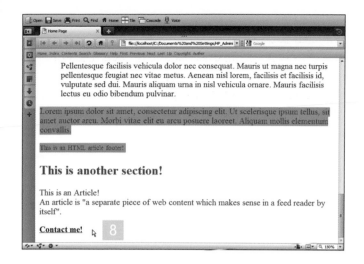

Creating a hyperlink to an e-mail address (cont.)

8 Save the HTML file and open it in a web browser, then click the hyperlink in the page footer to launch your default mail program with the fields populated and the body text in the message.

4

HTML hyperlinks 79

Adding images to an HTML page

5

Introduction

Images on the Internet have come a long way since the early days of the World Wide Web. At one time, technology limitations hindered the use and scope of images, as well as how they could be displayed. Now, computer hardware can show images with millions of colour variations, play videos streamed over broadband connections, share and display photographs of almost unlimited dimensions on sites such as Flickr and Google Photos, and so much more.

Gone are the days of VGA or XGA monitors, tiny screen resolutions and weak video cards. Today's computers are graphics-dependent and the Internet is moving away from a text-only library of pages to a multimedia experience unlike anything seen before. To make your web page stand out from the millions, you need to know how to work with graphics and photographs and get them on to your pages.

For the most part, the images you'll work with on web pages come in three formats.

■ **JPEG (Joint Photographic Experts Group format)** This is the standard format for graphics with many and subtle variations and is the best native format on the Internet for photographs. Whenever you use photos as part of a web page, make sure they are in JPEG format. JPEG images have the file extension .jpg or .jpeg.

What you'll do

Add images to a web page

Create image links

Create thumbnail image links

Create an Image map

Mark up an image as a figure

■ **GIF (Graphics Interchange Format)** This was a standard for static, non-photographic images and line art at one time. It has largely fallen out of use, but is still the native format for animated GIF images (those images which are animated and often used as avatars or icons). Animated GIF images are generally composed of several images scrolled or rotated one after another in rapid succession, forming a crude animation. GIF files use the .gif extension.

■ **PNG (Portable Network Graphics format)** This is the modern standard for artwork on the Internet. It has tremendous colour capabilities and good image file size properties. PNG files also allow for advanced features, such as transparency. PNG files use the extension .png.

Important

While most modern browsers take full advantage of the existing advanced features of the PNG format, older browsers may not allow for all of them, such as adaptive transparency.

The rule of thumb is to use JPEGs for photos, PNG for art and GIFs for animated GIF images.

A high-resolution image can be huge, in both its file size and physical dimensions. When dealing with Internet pages, designing for screen resolutions lower than 1024 by 768 pixels isn't necessary, but, to see the image on the screen without using scroll bars or reducing the browser's zoom view, avoid using large files or include a thumbnail of the full image users can click to see it full-sized.

There is good news and bad news for this task. The good news is you will learn how to add images to a web page. The bad news is no you won't.

What that means is, there really isn't any way actually to add images to a *web page*. Unlike a word processing program or desktop publishing software, an HTML file is just *text*. All text, all the time. In order for images to be shown, we have to point the browser to the image and ask it to display the image in the correct place on the page. This is done with the image (`<img>`) tag.

Table 5.1 Tag used in this task

Tag	Function
`<img/>`	Specifies the location of an image on a web page. The **src** attribute is used to specify the location of the image file. The **width** attribute specifies the image's width, while the **height** attribute specifies its height. The **alt** attribute provides alternative text in the event the image can't be viewed.

To tell the browser where to display an image, we must provide two things. The first is the image we want to display. This is done in the **src** attribute of the `<img>` tag. The value must be a valid URL, absolute or relative, for the image to show. The second thing we must provide is the spot on the page where the image will be which is done with `<img>` element placement.

Note that the `<img>` tag isn't an element, but a standalone tag. What this means is there is no end tag. Instead a trailing forward slash is used at the end of the start tag.

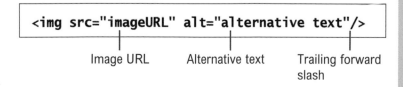

Image URL   Alternative text   Trailing forward slash

Adding images to a web page (cont.)

In this task, you will place an image in your Main Folder and add an `<img>` element to the main page to show the image. You will also create alternative text in the event a visitor cannot view the image and give the image a title. The results of the task are visible and obvious and show how easy it is to place images on a web page.

1 Download or locate images to use on your sample web page and copy or save them to the same folder as your sample web page.

2 Open your sample web page in your text editor and save it with a new name.

3 Locate the 'Lorem ipsum' paragraph in the first `<article>`. Find the `<blockquote>` element in the paragraph. After the start tag for the block quote element, add an `<img>` element. In the `src` attribute, list the name and, if appropriate, the location of the first image you want to show on the page. In the `<alt>` attribute, give a brief (one or two words, if possible) description of the image.

4 Immediately after the `<blockquote>` element's end tag, include another image using the `<img>` tag with `src` and `alt` tags included.

! Important

In this task, you will use either your own images or graphics or ones from the Internet. To avoid any and all copyright infringement, please make sure you have permission from the image owner to use any images you choose for the exercise. While you will not be publishing the web pages you create to the Internet at this time, it is still best practice to secure the permission of the image's creator for use before downloading anything. I chose to use the sample pictures provided with my copy of Windows on my computer.

For your information

Since the task using hyperlinks has been completed, you can remove the hyperlinks from your sample page if you like. If you want to leave them in place and have them remain functional, either save the Index.htm file in your Main Folder, save it to a new location and update the link URLs in your sample page or save it in a new location with the subfolder and both subpages.

3

```
32   <p>Lorem ipsum dolor sit amet, consectetur adipiscing elit. Nullam cursus feugiat
     consectetur. Duis fringilla enim at sem fermentum id dignissim sapien commodo.
     Quisque nisl sapien, malesuada non varius sed, fringilla sit amet sapien. Duis ac
     felis ante. <blockquote><img src="At the Arch.jpg" alt="A Stone Arch"/>Pellentesque
     facilisis vehicula dolor nec consequat. Mauris ut magna nec turpis pellentesque
     feugiat nec vitae metus. Aenean nisl lorem, facilisis et facilisis id, vulputate sed
     dui. Mauris aliquam urna in nisl vehicula ornare. Mauris facilisis lectus eu odio
     bibendum pulvinar.</blockquote> <img src="Sunset.jpg" alt="A lovely sunset"/>Lorem
     ipsum dolor sit amet, consectetur adipiscing elit. Ut scelerisque ipsum tellus, sit
     amet auctor arcu. Morbi vitae elit eu arcu posuere laoreet. Aliquam mollis elementum
     convallis.</p>
```

4

Important

If the image you chose is large (the one I used for this example was *huge*), you can alter the size with photo-editing software. Some very good (and free) image-editing software packages are GIMP (the Gnu Image Manipulation Program) and Paint.net (an upgraded, Windows-specific version of the venerable Paint program included with Windows). You can do a Google search for free image editing software to find others as well.

5 Save the HTML file and open it in your web browser to observe the results.

For your information

The pictures added to the web page are not positioned by the location of the <img> tag alone. CSS can be used to wrap text around the image, place the image more precisely on the page and align the image horizontally and vertically with surrounding content.

Creating image links

1 Download or locate a series of images you are free to use for this task and save them to your Main Folder. Be sure the names do not conflict with the names you gave the images in the previous task.

2 Open your sample web page in your text editor and save it with a new name in your Main Folder.

3 Locate the `<aside>` element. Delete all the text contents of the `<ul>` element but leave the `<ul>` and `<li>` elements themselves in place (unless you don't mind retyping them).

4 In the first list element, add an `<img>` tag and include the `src` and `alt` attributes for the first image you want to use as a hyperlink.

5 Around the `<img>` tag, create an anchor element which opens a favourite web page of your choosing. If you like, set the target attribute to open in a new tab or window.

In some cases, it may be desirable to create a hyperlink from an image rather than from text. This is simple and easy to accomplish. Instead of surrounding *text* with an anchor element (`<a>...</a>`), surround an *image* with one.

Some browsers will place a blue border around the image when you create an image hyperlink. The border is to notify the user of the hyperlink. You can eliminate the border with CSS.

Important

Not all browsers will put the border around an image and the colour of the border will depend on your personal browser settings. If you've changed the colour of unvisited hyperlinks in the settings, the border will appear as whatever colour you set.

The results of this task are straightforward. A series of images with borders around them should appear on your sample web page, indicating the images are hyperlinks. Simply click each image at the end to test the hyperlinks.

```
14  <aside style="color:blue">        I
15  <h2>This is the sidebar</h2>
16  <var>This is the sidebar content</var>. <ul><li><a href=
    "http://www.Google.com/"><img src="Big Wave.jpg" alt="Big wave"/></a></li>
    <li><a href="http://uk.yahoo.com"><img src="At the Arch.jpg" alt="Stone arch"/>
    </a></li> <li><a href="http://www.amazon.co.uk"><img src="Sunset.jpg" alt=
    "Sunset"/></a></li> <li><a href="www.wikipedia.org"><img src="Blue Hills.jpg"
    alt="Blue hills"/></a></li></ul>
17  </aside>
```

Cross reference

See Chapter 4 to refresh your memory on how to set `href` and `target` attributes for an anchor element if you need to.

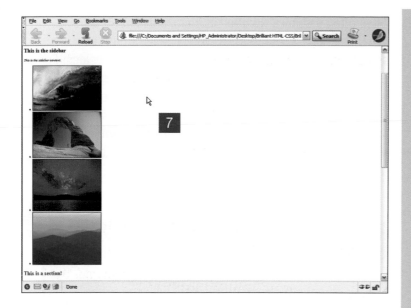

6 Repeat this process for all
   four list item elements in
   the `<ul>` element, using
   a unique `img` and `alt`
   attribute for each.

7 Save the HTML file and open
   it in your web browser.

Note the Opera™ browser,
and Safari for Macs, does
not add the blue border to
link images.

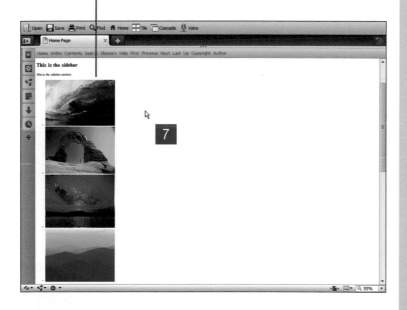

Creating thumbnail image links

Sites often display a number of images in thumbnail size. When you click these images, you're taken to full-sized versions of them or to the site where the image resides. For example, think about Google. Do a search for some term and, when the results list appears, click the Images link just below your toolbar. The page will display all the images related to your search term in thumbnail form. When you click a thumbnail, you will be taken to the source of that image or a full-sized version.

For your information

When using Google to search for images, when you click a thumbnail image, a frameset will load in the browser. The image will be in the bottom frame and the top one will be the Google thumbnail. This is one modern example of a page which still uses frames to display content.

An image's width and height are set with the `<img>` tag height and width attributes. They change the size of the displayed image on the screen, but not its actual file size. They are set in pixels using integer values. The values must be kept in the same aspect ratio or else the picture will appear distorted.

Jargon buster

Integer – A whole, non-fractional, non-decimal number.

Aspect ratio – The ratio of width to height for a visual element, such as a video or image.

When you've finished this task, your sample page will have a thumbnail image which links to a subpage with the full-sized image on it. When you click the thumbnail image, the subpage should load in a new window or tab.

```
21 ┌ <h2>This is a section!</h2>
22 │ <p><a href="Subpage1.htm" target="_blank"><img src="Big Wave.jpg" height="50"
 3 │ width="50" alt="Big wave icon"/></a><em>Lorem ipsum dolor sit amet</em>,
   │ consectetur adipiscing elit. Nullam cursus feugiat consectetur. Duis fringilla
   │ enim at sem fermentum id dignissim sapien commodo. Quisque nisl sapien,
   │ malesuada non varius sed, <i>fringilla sit amet sapien</i>. Duis ac felis
   │ ante. Pellentesque facilisis vehicula dolor nec consequat. Mauris ut magna nec
   │ turpis pellentesque feugiat nec vitae metus. Aenean nisl lorem, facilisis et
   │ facilisis id, vulputate sed dui. <strong>Mauris aliquam urna in nisl vehicula
   │ ornare</strong>. Mauris facilisis lectus eu odio bibendum pulvinar. Lorem
   │ ipsum dolor sit amet, consectetur adipiscing elit. Ut scelerisque ipsum
   │ tellus, sit amet auctor arcu. Morbi vitae elit eu arcu posuere laoreet.
   │ Aliquam mollis <b>elementum convallis</b>.</p>
```

For your information

The `alt` attribute offers a text alternative when a browser cannot load an image. It's good practice to always have the `alt` attribute set, but it does not have any impact on whether the image does or does not display or on its appearance in any way.

Important

The picture will likely be distorted on viewing. This is to be expected unless you use an image with the same dimensions for both height and width because the aspect ratio is not the same as the original image.

Creating thumbnail image links (cont.)

1 Open your sample web page in your text editor and save it with a new name in your Main Folder.

2 Locate the first 'Lorem ipsum' paragraph. Before the first `<em>` element, add an `<img>` tag and set the `src` attribute to an image of your choosing. If you like, set the `alt` attribute to 'Image thumbnail'.

3 Set the height and width attributes to 50.

4 Wrap the `<img>` tag with an anchor element. Set the `href` attribute to "`Subpage1.htm`" and set the target to `_blank`.

5 Save the HTML file.

6 Open Subpage 1.htm in your text editor and add an `<img>` tag to the page anywhere you'd like, then save and close the file.

5

Creating thumbnail image links (cont.)

7 Open the homepage and click on the thumbnail link to launch the Subpage one web page.

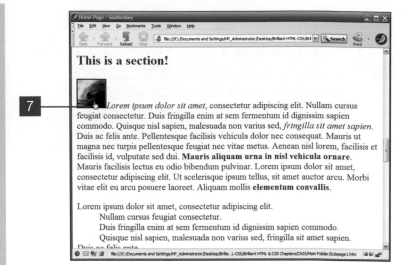

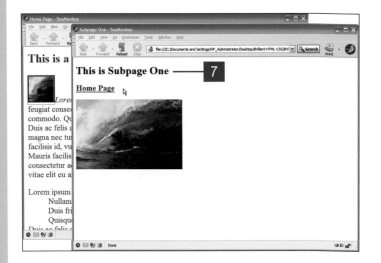

An image map is a graphic or picture which has navigational sections to it. For example, you might have a world map with clickable sections for North America, South America, Europe–Middle East–Africa and Asia–Pacific areas. Clicking each of the four sections would open an area-specific page or site.

Creating an image map

Or, imagine we're at the supermarket again. This time, instead of a shopping list on our computer screen, we have an image of a cornucopia. The image has breads, cheeses, milk, fruits and vegetables, meats and a big stack of boxes all spilling out of the horn o' plenty. Each of the items is a clickable spot on the image. By clicking the bread, you're taken to the bread aisle. By clicking the milk, you're taken to the dairy section. By clicking the fruits or vegetables, you go to the shop's fruit and vegetable section and so on.

Jargon buster

Hotspot – A clickable section of an image or object on a web page. Clicking the hotspot triggers an event of some kind – usually a navigational hyperlink to another resource or section of the current resource.

Image map – An image divided into clickable areas, or hotspots, which often function as navigational links to other resources or sections of a resource.

The hyperlinks in an image map are no different from the hyperlinks in a `<nav>` element, except they use a portion of an *image* rather than *text* for the clickable link.

Any image can be used as an image map. Simply tell the browser the image is a map, which portions are hyperlinks and where they are to link to.

5

Creating an image map (cont.)

1. Open your sample web page in the text editor and save it in your Main Folder with a new name.

2. Select a picture to use as your image map. For convenience and to make it easy on yourself to complete this task, choose an image which can be easily divided into quadrants. A clock or map of the globe works well for this purpose.

3. Create a rough sketch of the image and divide the sketch into four regions or quadrants. These will become your hotspots.

Table 5.2 Tags used in this task

Tag	Function
`<map>...</map>`	Specifies an image map. The `<img/>` tag's `usemap` attribute must match a hash name in the `name` attribute of a `<map>` element.
`<area>...</area>`	Specifies a portion of an image to be used as a hyperlink. The `href` attribute must be included in order for it to be a hyperlink.

Creating an image map requires you to take three basic steps. First, determine the image dimensions in pixels. Second, determine which areas of the image will be hotspots. Finally, put all the information together in `<map>` and `<area>` elements using an `<img/>` tag to place the image and the `usemap` attribute to name the map.

In this task you will create an image map using one of your own images or one from the Internet (and, of course, you will be careful only to use images for which permission has been granted for use, ahem!). On completion, you will have four different hotspots which link to external websites. If you hold your mouse pointer over each quadrant of the image, you'll notice the status bar of your Internet browser changes to the URL of the resource to which you linked. You can test the links by clicking each one.

! Important

It is critical that you know the dimensions, in pixels, of your image. You can use many different programs to help you find out, including Paint. Open the image in Paint, then go to the **Image** menu and choose **Attributes**. The image's dimensions will be displayed on the screen in the dialogue box. Choose **Pixels** for the unit if it hasn't already been selected. Write down the image dimensions so you have them to hand.

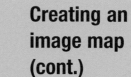
Cross reference

See the HTML comments task in Chapter 1 to review HTML comments.

Creating an image map (cont.)

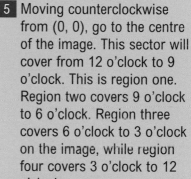

4 Locate the `<nav>` element and place a comment around the entire element.

5 Moving counterclockwise from (0, 0), go to the centre of the image. This sector will cover from 12 o'clock to 9 o'clock. This is region one. Region two covers 9 o'clock to 6 o'clock. Region three covers 6 o'clock to 3 o'clock on the image, while region four covers 3 o'clock to 12 o'clock.

6 In the sample page HTML file, add an `<img/>` tag. Set the `src` attribute for the image you're using for your image map. Set the `alt` attribute as 'Image map' and add the `usemap` attribute with the setting `"#world-map"`.

7 Under the `<img/>` tag, add a `<map>` element. Set the name element to `"world-map"`.

5

Creating an image map (cont.)

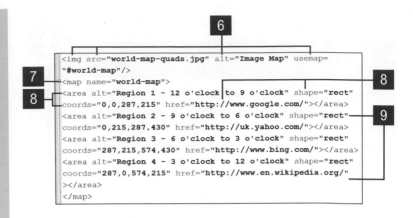

```
<img src="world-map-quads.jpg" alt="Image Map" usemap=
"#world-map"/>
<map name="world-map">
<area alt="Region 1 - 12 o'clock to 9 o'clock" shape="rect"
coords="0,0,287,215" href="http://www.google.com/"></area>
<area alt="Region 2 - 9 o'clock to 6 o'clock" shape="rect"
coords="0,215,287,430" href="http://uk.yahoo.com/"></area>
<area alt="Region 3 - 6 o'clock to 3 o'clock" shape="rect"
coords="287,215,574,430" href="http://www.bing.com/"></area>
<area alt="Region 4 - 3 o'clock to 12 o'clock" shape="rect"
coords="287,0,574,215" href="http://www.en.wikipedia.org/"
></area>
</map>
```

8 Inside the `map` element, add four `<area>` elements. In the first, add the `alt` attribute with the value **"Region 1 – 12 o'clock to 9 o'clock"**. Set the shape attribute to **"rect"** and the `coords` attribute to go from (0, 0) to the centre of the left-hand edge (your coordinates will depend on the image dimensions). Finally, set the `href` attribute to "**http://www. google.com/**".

9 Repeat this process for the other three `<area>` elements, setting the `coords` attributes to correspond to regions two, three and four respectively. Set region two to link to **"http://uk.yahoo.com/"**, region three to link to **"http:// www.bing.com/"** and region four to link to **"http://www. en.wikipedia.org"**.

10 Save the HTML file, open it in your browser and test the hotspots by clicking each one.

Occasionally, it might be necessary to include an image on a web page as a figure for text content, such as you might find with a mathematical discussion or an illustrated page where text refers to specific images. HTML5 provides new ways to include not just the figure but the caption for it as well.

Table 5.3 Tags used in this task

Tag	Function
`<figure>`… `</figure>`	Designates content which is represented as a figure and referred to in the main content areas. A 'figure' can be textual content or an image, video or other media content.
`<figcaption>`… `</figcaption>`	Designates content which is used as the caption for a figure. The `<figcaption>` element must be either the first or last child element of the `<figure>` element. Only one figure caption is permitted per figure.

To designate content as a figure, simply encapsulate it with the `<figure>` element. To include the figure's caption, add the `<figcaption>` element with the text content to designate it as the caption which goes with that figure.

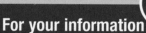

For your information

You can use multiple images for figures, just enclose them all in the `<figure>` element. The `<figcaption>` element, if used, must either come before any other figure content or last, after all the other figure content. Each `<figure>` element can have only one `<figcaption>` element.

Jargon buster

Child element – An HTML element which is nested inside another HTML element containing content directly related to the *parent* element.

Parent element – An HTML element which contains other directly related HTML elements and content.

5

Marking up an image as a figure (cont.)

The results of this task are simple and clear. You will use the image map created in the previous task, identifying it now as Figure 1 and create a caption to go along with it. Note afterwards how different browsers render the image slightly differently. Opera™ shows the figure caption to the lower right of the image, while Mozilla's SeaMonkey renders the blue border around the image map and places the figure caption directly beneath and aligned to the left side of the figure.

1 Open the sample web page in your text editor and save it with a new name in your Main Folder.

2 Locate the image map you created in the previous task.

3 Before the `<img>` tag, add the `<figure>` tag.

4 After the `</map>` tag, add the `<figcaption>` element with the content 'The Image Map for External Links'.

5 After the `</figcaption>` tag, add the `</figure>` tag.

6 Save the HTML file and open it in more than one browser to view the differences in the way they display the results.

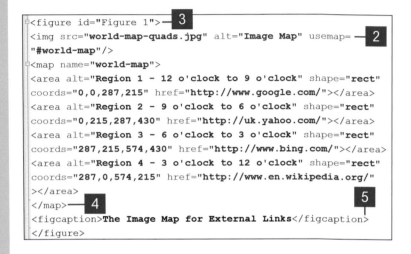

```
<figure id="Figure 1">━3
<img src="world-map-quads.jpg" alt="Image Map" usemap=━2
"#world-map"/>
<map name="world-map">
<area alt="Region 1 - 12 o'clock to 9 o'clock" shape="rect"
coords="0,0,287,215" href="http://www.google.com/"></area>
<area alt="Region 2 - 9 o'clock to 6 o'clock" shape="rect"
coords="0,215,287,430" href="http://uk.yahoo.com/"></area>
<area alt="Region 3 - 6 o'clock to 3 o'clock" shape="rect"
coords="287,215,574,430" href="http://www.bing.com/"></area>
<area alt="Region 4 - 3 o'clock to 12 o'clock" shape="rect"
coords="287,0,574,215" href="http://www.en.wikipedia.org/"
></area>
</map>━4                                              5
<figcaption>The Image Map for External Links</figcaption>
</figure>
```

HTML tables

Introduction

As long as there has been tabular data to present, there have been ways to present it ... and the Internet is no different. Tabular data on the Internet is displayed using, logically enough, HTML tables.

> **Jargon buster**
>
> **Tabular data** – Data which is presented in table format – that is, in a series of rows and columns.

Tables, whether in HTML or otherwise, consist of columns and rows which are made up of cells to house individual data or content. The content need not be numerical or statistical. Tables can also contain images, multimedia content, resources from the Internet, such as different pages from the same site or hyperlinks to other sites, and more. In fact, table cells can hold pretty much anything.

Because they can hold anything, HTML tables can do more than just display tabular data. They can also be used to perform page layout tasks. They have great flexibility and, when framesets became too cumbersome to work with, tables took over as the layout tool of choice for designing web pages. Sectioning with tables makes setting up the layout easy and much more efficient, not to mention attractive, than using framesets.

What you'll do

Create an HTML table

Adjust the padding and spacing in a table's cells

Create table headings

Add a caption to a table

Form the body of a table

Span cells across rows and columns

Create a table footer

HTML tables are built using tags which form rows and cells. Specific cells can span both rows and columns to create larger divisions of the space. Some HTML table formatting aspects – such as borders, cell padding and cell spacing (which are covered in more detail later in this chapter) – can be handled using the `<table>` element's attributes. Many attributes for formatting inline have been deprecated, however, and so are no longer in use. Like other formatting duties, most table formatting has been moved to CSS as it can do a better job.

Many table elements are optional and some can be used more than once in a table. For example, a table can have a `<thead>` element to signify a table head, but only one. Likewise, a table can have a `<tfoot>` element to designate the table footer, but, again, only one. On the other hand, a table can contain one or more `<colgroup>` elements, which are used to group some column elements together.

In this chapter's tasks, you will learn how to create a table and format its parts. You will also experiment with using a table for basic layout purposes with our empty HTML template from Chapter 1.

An HTML table has descending layers of construction, just as a web page does. To create an HTML table, the first element you need is the `<table>...</table>` element.

This doesn't automatically create the table for you in the way that Microsoft Word or OpenOffice.org Writer would. It simply places the table element to designate the area in which the table resides. The browser will then be aware that the elements and tags you add after it are all part of that table.

Table 6.1 Tags used in this task

Tag	Function
`<table>...` `</table>`	Specifies an HTML table.
`<tr>...</tr>`	Signifies an HTML table row.
`<td>...</td>`	Signifies an HTML table data cell.

The next thing necessary for a table is a set of rows. An HTML table row is marked up using the `<tr>...</tr>` element.

Each row of an HTML table is comprised of a series of horizontal table data cells which contain the actual data. The cells are signified by the `<td>...</td>` element.

The hierarchy of elements, then, is the table element (`<table>...</table>`), which contains all the other elements of the table. The table row element (`<tr>...</tr>`) contains the table data cells. The table data cells (`<td>...</td>`) contain the actual data to display in the table.

The creation of an HTML table is straightforward and the markup is easy to read, as you will discover in this task. You will open a new web page, create a table with four rows and three columns and view the results in your browser. It will appear like a small, waffle-type figure in the upper left-hand corner of the screen. In subsequent tasks, you will add data and other elements to this table.

Creating an HTML table

6

For your information

An HTML table can have other elements along with the table row and table data cell elements. Some of them are discussed in other tasks later in this chapter.

Creating an HTML table (cont.)

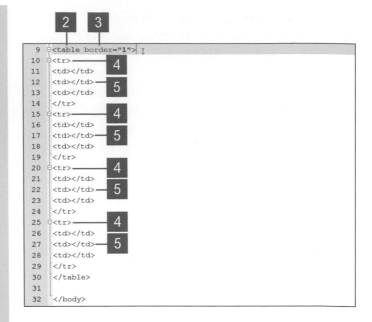

1 Open the HTML template you created in Chapter 1 in your text editor and save it with a new name.

2 In the **<body>** element add a table (**<table>…</table>**) element.

3 In the start tag, add **border="1"** to set the border width to 1 pixel.

4 In the **<table>** element, add four table row (**<tr>…</tr>**) elements.

5 Within each of the table row elements, add three table data (**<td>…</td>**) elements.

6 Save the HTML file and open it in your web browser.

i For your information

The value of the **border** attribute is *understood* to be in pixels, so no unit needs to be entered. If no border is desired, the attribute would be simply omitted, not set to **"0"**.

i For your information

The preferred method for setting the pixel width for table borders is with CSS, not with this deprecated **<table>** element attribute. If we do not set this attribute now, however, the table may not be visible in all browsers.

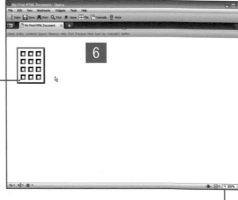

Note the magnification for this image is set to 500% of normal so the image is more clearly visible. Your table, without data in it, will be much smaller on the screen. In fact, only 20% of this size.

Cell padding and cell spacing refer to the white space in a table. White space is critical to the legibility of content and tables, with their rules and borders, are especially prone to cluttering and becoming unclear. Use of cell padding and spacing helps alleviate problems in data presentation in a table with all its horizontal rules or one in which all the gridlines are present.

The terms cell padding and cell spacing can be confusing if you're not familiar with them. Cell padding refers to the white space *inside* a cell – that is, the space between the cell walls and the content. Cell spacing refers to the distance between the cells themselves.

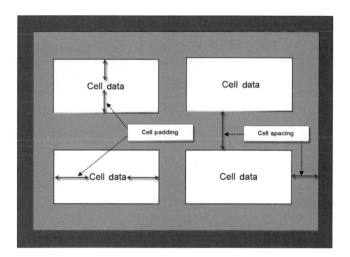

For your information

There are other ways to control white space and legibility of data in a table. For instance, using only some of the rules rather than all the gridlines can greatly clarify tabular presentation. As with all other aspects of HTML, formatting of borders and white space are best left to CSS, but a discussion of cell padding and spacing in the construction of a table is important as then you can use all available information and decide how best to present the data.

Important

!

Knowing how to adjust the white space in a table can be helpful, but most formatting of tables is done using CSS now. This task has been included here, though, to further your table design knowledge.

Cell padding is controlled in HTML using the `cellpadding` attribute of the `<table>` element's start tag. Cell spacing is controlled by means of the `cellspacing` attribute.

Adjusting the padding and spacing in a table's cells (cont.)

1. Open the HTML file you worked on in the last task in your text editor and save it with a new name.

2. In the `<table>` element's start tag, add the attribute `cellpadding="10"` after the border width.

3. In the `<table>` element's start tag, add the attribute `cellspacing="20"` after the cellpadding attribute.

4. Save the file and open it in your web browser to view the results.

Important

While the attributes for cell padding and spacing are deprecated, they still function. This is true of many other deprecated attributes as well. It is good practice, therefore, to not form a habit of using those attributes, but knowing they're there if needed is handy.

This task is simple and the results are immediately visible. You will increase the white space in the table using the table attributes `cellpadding` and `cellspacing` and then reduce it to emphasise the effect the adjustments have made. While this isn't likely to be an exercise you will encounter during actual web page design, it is helpful to know what the ramifications are for CSS properties later in the book.

```
8
9  <table border="1" cellpadding="10" cellspacing="20">
10 <tr>
11 <td></td>
```

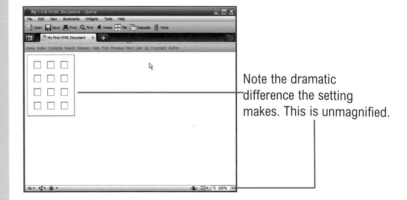

Note the dramatic difference the setting makes. This is unmagnified.

Table headings are rows or groups of rows used as column and row titles. Generally, a header describes the tabular data it heads. The text might be bold or emphasised in other ways to make it stand out from the tabular data itself.

Table headers are marked up in a couple of different ways in HTML, depending on the type of heading.

Table 6.2 Tags used in this task

Tag	Function
`<thead>...</thead>`	Designates a table row or group of rows as a table header.
`<th>...</th>`	Designates a header cell within a table row.

Deciding which element to use to create the right heading is easy. If you want to create a row header, where the header is for the row rather than the column, use the `<th>...</th>` element to designate the heading. To create a row or multiple rows for column headings use the `<thead>...</thead>` to enclose the rows to be used.

After completing the task below, you can view the results in your browser. You should be able to see a table on your web page with headings. You will also create a row heading for a few of the rows in the table and used the ` ` special character as a placeholder in blank cells, too. While the cells will seem a bit jumbled, the task clearly shows how table headings are used.

Creating table headings

6

For your information

Row headings are generally at the far left of the row they head. Both row and column headings can be used to create a grid, such as sales figures tracked year-on-year on a quarterly basis. In such cases, the use of empty cells as placeholders is beneficial.

A non-breaking space is a special character you can use in a cell which causes the character not to display but isn't seen as empty by the browser. A non-breaking space is created using the ampersand symbol (`&`) followed by the characters `nbsp` and a semi-colon, thus ` `.

Creating table headings (cont.)

1 Open the sample web page you created in the last task in your text editor and save it with a new name.

2 In the `<table>` element, remove the padding and spacing details, but leave the `border` attribute.

3 In the next, first row, change the `<tr>` element to `<thead>`. Don't forget to change the end tag as well.

4 In the first cell, add the non-breaking space special character designator (` `).

5 In the other cells, insert the content 'First Quarter' and 'Second Quarter'.

6 In the second row, change the first `<td>` element to a `<th>` element.

7 In the header cell, add the year '2008'.

8 Add data to the rest of the row.

9 Repeat this process for each subsequent row, using '2009' and '2010' as the row headings and filling in the rest of the cells with data.

10 Save the HTML file and open it in your web browser to view the results.

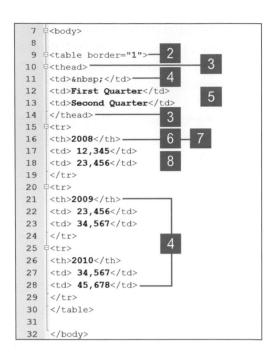

For your information

I have used values with sequential numbers for simplicity, but you can use any data equally well.

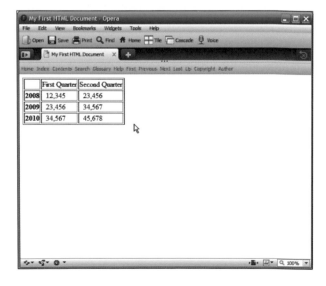

When using a table as an illustrative figure along with other content, it's often necessary to name it. Giving the table a name or title – a caption – is easy using the `<caption>…</caption>` element.

The `<caption>` element must be the first element in the `<table>` element when it's used. If you use *other* elements before the `<caption>` element within the `<table>` element, the caption for the table will not be displayed.

Table 6.3 Tag used in this task

Tag	Function
`<caption>…` `</caption>`	Designates the title of a table, which is its parent element.

The `<caption>` element can contain more than just the title of the table, though. For example, if you wanted to have something about the table or the data appear in the caption along with the title, other elements, such as the `<p>` element, can be used inside the `<caption>` element:

```
<caption>Table 1.1

<p>This table represents the annual
growth rate for peanuts fertilized with
ground tarantulas in the Amazon basin
for the last five years.</p>

</caption>
```

The caption element may format the caption text, depending on browser interpretation. In my version of Opera[TM], for example, the text was centred directly under the caption title. The entire caption in turn was centred directly above the table for which it provided the caption.

Adding a caption to a table

Important

Remember, the `<caption>` element doesn't apply specific formatting. It tells the browser how it should interpret the content in the tag. The interpretation of that tag is left to the browser manufacturer. It is possible, though unlikely, that Opera[TM], Internet Explorer and Safari will all interpret the same tag differently. The example given by the WHATWG for the `<caption>` element does not show the text being centred, but does show it being reduced in size and italicised. These changes did not manifest themselves in my browser versions. So, don't expect any specific type of formatting, unless you apply it yourself to the text content.

Adding a caption to a table (cont.)

In this task you will add the `<caption>` element to your table and textual descriptive content as well, using the `<p>` element and the `<h5>` element within the `<caption>` element. The results will show a minor heading title and the paragraph of text added to the table as a caption.

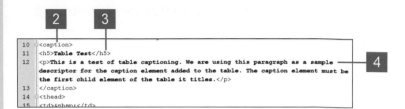

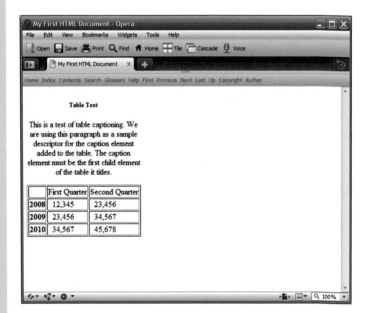

1 Open the sample web page from the previous task in your text editor and save it with a new name.

2 Under the `<table>` element and before the `<thead>` start tag, add the `<caption>` element.

3 In the caption element, add an `<h5>` element with the content 'Table Test'. Don't forget to close the `<h5>` element.

4 Add a `<p>` element and some descriptive text. Only a few lines are necessary (you may use 'Lorem ipsum' text if you'd like). Don't forget to add the end tag for the `<p>` element.

5 Save the HTML file and load it in your web browser to view the results.

So far, if you've worked through the tasks in this chapter in order, you will have created a table, adjusted the white space in it, added a heading or two and inserted a caption. All of these things takes place outside the main body of the table.

HTML allows you to designate a block of rows and columns as the body of the table, using the `<tbody>` element.

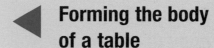
Table 6.4 Tag used in this task

Tag	Function
`<tbody>...</tbody>`	Specifies the body of an HTML table.

The `<tbody>` element must come after the `<caption>` and `<thead>` elements in a table (if they're used), but before any `<tr>` elements used outside of headings. It contains zero or more `<tr>` elements and must come before any table footer element (`<tfooter>...</tfooter>`) used.

Cross reference

See the task 'Creating a table footer' later in this chapter for more information on the `<tfooter>` element.

In this task, you will enclose a group of rows and designate them as the data body of the table in a `<tbody>` element. The results of the task, however, are to aid the clarity of the markup and grouping and make formatting easy with CSS, but have no HTML visual effect. Adding a deprecated attribute assists with the visual clarity, however.

Forming the body of a table (cont.)

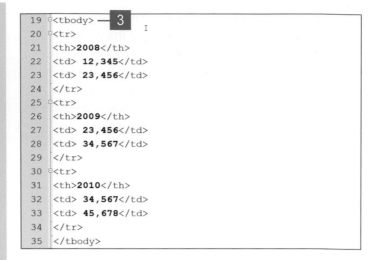

1 Open the sample web page from the previous task in your text editor and save it with a new name.

2 Find the `<thead>` element end tag and add a blank line beneath it.

3 Type the `<tbody>` start tag in the newly created blank line.

4 Locate the `</table>` tag and add a blank line after it.

5 In the newly created blank line, type the `<thead>` end tag (`</thead`).

6 Save the HTML file and open it in your web browser.

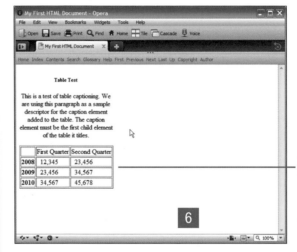

Notice there is no visual change after adding the `<tbody>` element to the table.

For your information

Don't be surprised when you see no change in your table's appearance. The `<thead>` element doesn't have any visual effect unless it's formatted with CSS.

It may be necessary to have a single cell within a table span more than one column or row, or both, within a table. Headings with subheadings, for example, or one division with two subdivisions in two separate columns, create situations where a heading cell must span more than one column or row.

Spanning multiple columns or rows is achieved by using the `colspan` or `rowspan` attribute of either the `<th>` or `<td>` elements. Rows and columns can be spanned at will, but the correct number of rows and columns must be omitted or included whenever a cell spans for the structure to be correct.

Jargon buster

Column spanning – Crossing over multiple columns in a table with a single data cell.

Row spanning – Crossing over multiple rows in a table with a single data cell.

As with controlling the white space in a table, controlling row and column spanning permits you to make tables more visually appealing and present data more clearly.

For your information

The end tags for the `<tr>`, `<td>` and `<th>` elements are optional. It is not necessary to include them and, in fact, the code may be clarified in certain circumstances by omitting them. For the sake of establishing good habits and following best practice, however, end tags are used whenever they are optional in this book. In practice, you will decide for yourself what works best for you.

Spanning cells across rows and columns (cont.)

This task shows you how to span rows and columns with the `rowspan` and `colspan` attributes. The results will be clear in the resulting table. The empty cell in the upper left-hand corner of the table will then span two rows, while the column headers will span two columns each. Understanding how to span rows and columns allows you to create tables which are easy to read and interesting.

1 Open the sample web page you made in the previous task in your text editor and save it with a new name.

2 Locate the `<thead>` element of the table markup.

3 Add a `<tr>` element to wrap the `<td>` and `<th>` elements, which contain the non-breaking space (` `), 'First Quarter' and 'Second Quarter' content.

4 Add the attribute `rowspan="2"` to the `<td>` element, which has the non-breaking space.

5 Change the `<td>` element to a `<th>` element for the 'First Quarter' cell, then add the attribute `colspan="2"` to the start tag.

6 Do the same for the `<td>` element of the 'Second Quarter' cell.

7 Insert a `<tr>` element and, in the table row, add four `<th>` elements.

8 In the first new `<th>` element, add the content 'Cities'; in the second, add 'Suburbs'.

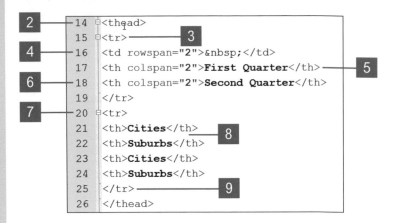

```
14  <thead>
15  <tr>
16    <td rowspan="2"> </td>
17    <th colspan="2">First Quarter</th>
18    <th colspan="2">Second Quarter</th>
19  </tr>
20  <tr>
21    <th>Cities</th>
22    <th>Suburbs</th>
23    <th>Cities</th>
24    <th>Suburbs</th>
25  </tr>
26  </thead>
```

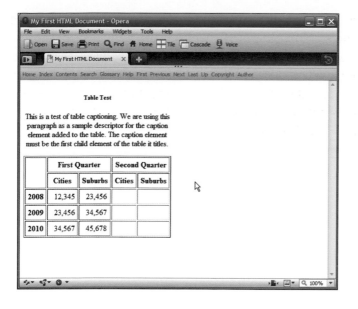

9 Do the same for the last two `<th>` elements also, then add the `<tr>` end tag for the new row.

10 Save the HTML file and open it in your web browser to review the results.

Creating a table footer

The last section of the table construct is the table footer. Table footers are blocks of rows which summarise information entered in the columns above them. Alternatively, they can be used as footnotes for tabular data.

Table 6.5 Tag used in this task

Tag	Function
`<tfoot>...</tfoot>`	Designates a row or group of rows as the table footer section in an HTML table.

Table footers display at the bottom of a table. The element must come after any `<thead>` or `<caption>` elements, but before a `<tbody>` element or any ungrouped `<tr>` elements in the table. The footer is specified by using the `<tfoot>` element and can contain any number of rows.

For your information

Because HTML tables do not *require* a footer, both the start and end tags for the `<tfoot>` element are considered and listed as optional in the World Wide Web Consortium's online documentation.

The results from this task are clear. After adding a `<tfoot>` element under the `<thead>` element, you will insert content into cells which span two columns. Despite their vertical location in the table markup in the HTML file, the browser will display the footer at the bottom of the table. Because the footer is contained in a separate element, specific formatting for the footer can be applied to the `<tfoot>` element for greater formatting control and visual impact.

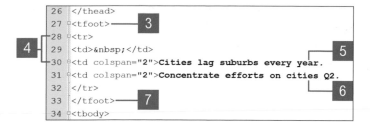

```
26  </thead>
27  <tfoot>————3
28  <tr>
29  <td> </td>
30  <td colspan="2">Cities lag suburbs every year.
31  <td colspan="2">Concentrate efforts on cities Q2.
32  </tr>
33  </tfoot>————7
34  <tbody>
```

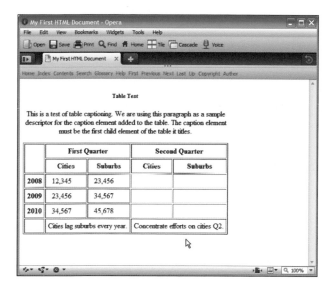

1. In your text editor, open the sample web page you made in the last task and save it with a new name.

2. Locate the `<thead>` element and add a couple of blank lines under the end tag for it.

3. In the new lines, type a `<tfoot>` element.

4. In the `<tfoot>` element, insert one row element and add three data cells in the row.

5. In the first `<td>` element, add a non-breaking space special character (` `). In the next `<td>` element, type the attribute `colspan="2"` into the start tag and add the content 'Cities lag suburbs every year'.

6. Repeat step 5 for the next `<td>` element, this time adding the cell content 'Concentrate efforts on cities Q2'.

7. Add the end tags for the `<tr>` and `<tfoot>` elements if you haven't yet.

8. Save the HTML file and open it in your web browser to view the results.

HTML forms

Introduction

If you've ever submitted any information over a website, you'll be no stranger to HTML forms. Many web pages gather information from users to store or use on other pages or site areas. Users provide the input via various controls on the form. The input is then used to order a product, set up an account, allow access to a site or resource and various other functions.

Jargon buster

Controls – Objects on an HTML form which receive input or settings from website users. Controls include objects such as dropdown lists or selection menus, 'radio' or option buttons, tick boxes (also called checkboxes), text fields, areas and more.

Web page forms house the controls which collect user data and transmit the gathered information to a web server for processing. Internet transactions are conducted millions of times a day and, in each of those transactions, HTML forms are probably involved.

Important

Some forms are not necessarily HTML forms as other programming or scripting languages are able to create forms dynamically and collect user input for processing by web servers.

What you'll do

Build a simple HTML form

Label HTML form controls

Add buttons to an HTML form

Add a selection box to an HTML form

Use HTML `<input />` controls

Add more HTML form controls

HTML5 provides form controls previously unavailable to web developers and designers without scripting or programming languages to supplement the page controls, such as JavaScript, VBScript, ASP, PHP, Perl and many others. These languages are generally used to customise functions and process data.

There are several steps required to set up an HTML form. Those steps can be performed in any order, but all must exist for the form to work – that is, gather the input from users, send it to the web server and have it processed and return results. Those steps are:

- create the user interface – that is, the environment the users providing the input will see and interact with
- set up the processing of the input on the web server
- establish communication between the user interface and web server.

Input data processing is not covered in this book as it is a big subject in itself, but we can still build a rudimentary form and have it accept input provided by users.

Building a basic HTML form is quick and easy. The problem is, you can't see that you've built an HTML form at all. A single element (along with various attributes and their values to provide the necessary functionality) informs the browser of the form's existence, but you can't see the results at all. So, to make the form visible and be able to interact with it a bit, we'll add a simple HTML text field to our form.

 Building a simple HTML form

Table 7.1 Tags used in this task

Tag	Function
`<form>...</form>`	Specifies an HTML form. Several available attributes are used to specify the functionality of the form itself.
`<fieldset>...</fieldset>`	Groups a set of form controls together under a single name.
`<legend>...</legend>`	Provides the name and label for a group of control elements in a `<fieldset>` element.
`<input />`	Specifies an HTML input control. The input tag is an empty tag – that is, there is only one tag used, similar to the `<img />` tag.

The HTML form itself is designated by the `<form>` element. All the other elements for the form are contained within it.

Think of the `<form>` element as being similar to the `<html>` element or as a grouping element, like the `<table>` element, which groups other elements like captions and footers. Essentially, the `<form>` element groups all the other form elements, such as controls, together. Form elements cannot be nested, but more than one may exist on an HTML page.

Building a simple HTML form (cont.)

Like most other HTML elements, the `<form>` element has several attributes which can be set in the start tag. The form's name, the `charset` attribute, and even `autocomplete` on or off can all be set by means of attributes in the `<form>` element's start tag. The attributes with which we will be most concerned in this task, however, are the `method` and `action` attributes.

The `method` attribute designates which protocol is used to send the data to the web server. While there are four settings for the `method` attribute, we will focus on only two: the `post` and `get` methods.

The `post` method tells the form to use the Post protocol, which means that the form puts all the data collected into a data packet with an HTTP header and sends the packet to the web server. The `get` method places all the data into a URL and transmits it to the web server in that format, which is known as the Get protocol.

HTML utilises the `<input>` element to great effect. There are many different types of input devices and HTML allows you to specify one within the `<type>` element of the `<input>` start tag. The control can also be named using the `name` attribute, while the number of characters it displays is controlled by the `size` attribute. Several controls on a form can also be given a common name using the `<fieldset>` element to group them. The `<legend>` element is used to provide the display name, which is similar to a `<caption>` element used for a table.

In this task, you will create a simple HTML form with two text fields for input, grouped together by a `<fieldset>` element and labelled using a `<legend>` element. On opening the page in a browser, you will clearly be able to see the new form, which will be modified in subsequent tasks.

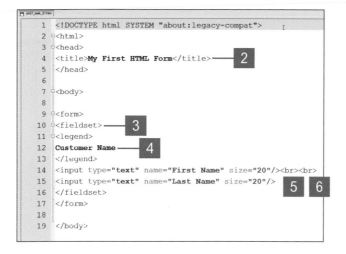

```
 1  <!DOCTYPE html SYSTEM "about:legacy-compat">
 2  <html>
 3  <head>
 4  <title>My First HTML Form</title>
 5  </head>
 6
 7  <body>
 8
 9  <form>
10  <fieldset>
11  <legend>
12  Customer Name
13  </legend>
14  <input type="text" name="First Name" size="20"/><br><br>
15  <input type="text" name="Last Name" size="20"/>
16  </fieldset>
17  </form>
18
19  </body>
```

1 Open your HTML template from Chapter 1 in your text editor and save it with a new name.

2 Change the `<title>` element content to 'My First HTML Form'. In the `<body>` element, add a `<form>` element.

3 In the new `<form>` element, add a `<fieldset>`.

4 In the `<fieldset>` element, add a `<legend>` element. Make the content of the element 'Customer Name'.

5 Beneath the `<legend>` element's end tag, add an `<input />` element. Set the `type` attribute to `"text"`, the `size` attribute to `"20"` and the name attribute to `"First Name"`.

6 After the first `<input />` element, add two `<br>` tags to create line breaks.

Important

The `<form>`, `<fieldset>` and `<legend>` elements all require an end tag as part of their construct. The `<input />` element is an empty element, meaning there is no closing tag. A trailing slash is used in the start tag, and the attributes are inserted before it to set the display for the browser.

For your information

If you do not add the line breaks between the `<input>` elements, they will both appear on the same line in the fieldset. You could also use `<p>` elements instead to create white space.

Building a simple HTML form (cont.)

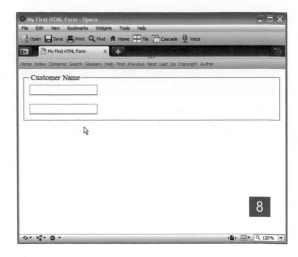

7. Beneath the first `<input>` element, add another one with the `type` attribute `"text"` and the `name` attribute `"Last Name"`.

8. Save the HTML file and open it in your web browser to view the results.

When you use many of the same type of form control on a form, it's also necessary to give users interacting with the form a clue as to what data needs to go into each one. For example, with our sample form from the last task, we told the browser to display an HTML form; we told the browser it should show two HTML text fields on the form; we told the form what the names of our text fields should be; and we told the browser those fields should be grouped into a fieldset with a common name. Users, however, will not see what those fields are called or know what sort of data they should put into them.

HTML provides the `<label>` element for this purpose. This is simply a label which appears on the web page for the control it's associated with. Users cannot interact with a label and a label does not return or receive any data – it's simply a sign with the name of the control on it. In other words, it's another form of caption.

Table 7.2 Tag used in this task

Tag	Function
`<label>...</label>`	Specifies a label for an HTML form object.

Labels can be explicitly associated with their forms or controls. If the `<label>` element's `form` attribute is set to the name of the form, it is said to be explicitly associated with the *form*. If the `form` attribute of the `<label>` element is set to the ID of the control it is associated with, it is said to be explicitly associated with the *control*.

None of that is necessary, but it may be useful on long pages with multiple forms for code clarity. For our purposes, we'll simply enclose the control we want to label with the `<label>` element, which will provide the results we want.

Labels are straightforward and simple. Once you have completed the following task, the labels on your form will be nicely captioned and the data types will be clear. We will use labels more in subsequent tasks, too.

Labelling HTML form controls

7

Important

A `<label>` element requires both a start and an end tag to indicate the label's content to the browser.

Labelling HTML form controls (cont.)

1 Open your sample web page from the previous task in your text editor and save it with a new name.

2 In the `<fieldset>` element, add the `<label>` element's start tag just before the first `<input>` element.

3 Before the `<input>` element, add the text 'First Name', followed by one or more non-breaking spaces and the `</label>` end tag. Be sure to add the end tag and content before the `<br>` tags.

4 Repeat the process in steps 2 and 3 above for the second `<input>` element, adding the label content 'Last Name'.

5 Save the HTML file and open it in your web browser to view the results.

Important

The label will appear according to where the text falls in the `<label>` element's content. So, if the `<input>` element precedes the text content, the label will be displayed to the *right* of the text box, but if it follows the text content (as in our task), the label will be displayed to the *left* of the text box. The blank space(s) are included to create white space between the label and the text box, and must be a special character non-breaking space (` `) to use more than one. Web browsers ignore space-bar generated spaces if more than one is used sequentially.

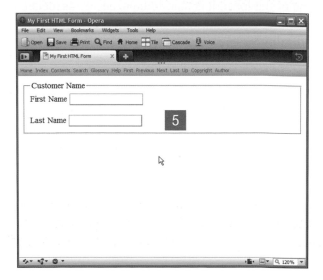

Button controls on HTML forms are specified by the `<button>` element. As with other HTML controls, they can be explicitly associated with their forms by means of attributes. Other attributes help to identify and label the buttons, as well as set how they behave. The buttons can even be disabled (or 'greyed out') on a form until certain conditions are met, such as certain fields having been populated or option buttons selected.

Table 7.3 Tag used in this task

Tag	Function
`<button>...</button>`	Specifies a button for an HTML form. The type of button is specified using the `type` attribute and the text content captured in the element is used as the text on the button itself.

Putting buttons on a form and making them do something are quite different matters. Adding buttons with the `<button>` element is simple, but having them perform actions is a bit more complex. In most cases, a scripting language controls what happens when buttons are clicked, but `type` attribute values enable the button to clear the form (a reset button) or submit the form data to the server (a submit button).

In our example, getting buttons to work isn't dependent entirely on the buttons themselves. It's also dependent on the form and the method/action assignment we provide. We must set the form's method and action attributes in order for the buttons to be able to do what they must do – in this case, send an e-mail using the `mailto:` protocol. Once the form's method and action have been set, we can use a submit button to send an e-mail.

In this task, you will create a 'Send' and a 'Reset' button. The reset button clears the form's fields of all data when clicked. The send button generates an e-mail message with a preformatted subject line.

Adding buttons to an HTML form

7

Jargon buster

Disabled – When a field or control on an HTML form, or a section of a form, is not available for user interaction. Generally, certain conditions must be met or data provided to enable the disabled control(s).

Important

Most HTML controls can be set to be disabled until certain conditions are met or other controls contain data.

Adding buttons to an HTML form (cont.)

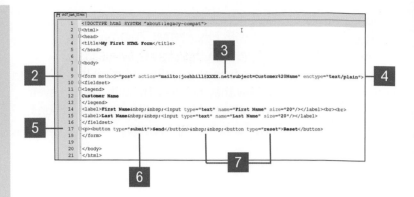

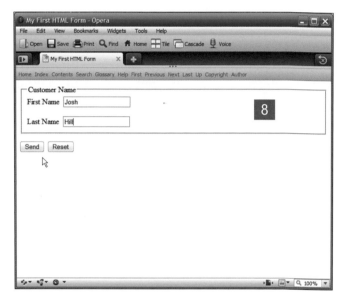

1. Open the sample web page from the previous task in your text editor and save it with a new name.

2. In the `<form>` element start tag, add the `method` attribute and set the value to `"post"`.

3. Add the `action` attribute and assign the value as `"mailto: youremailaddress@ email.com?subject= Customer%20Name"` (use your actual e-mail address if possible).

4. After the double quotes, add the `enctype` attribute to set the encryption type. Use the value `"text/plain"`. Enclose it in double quotes, as you have all other HTML attribute values.

5. Beneath the `</fieldset>` end tag, add a `<p>` element.

6. In the `<p>` element, add the `<button>` element. Set the `type` attribute to `"submit"`. Add the text 'Send' as the content between the start and end tags.

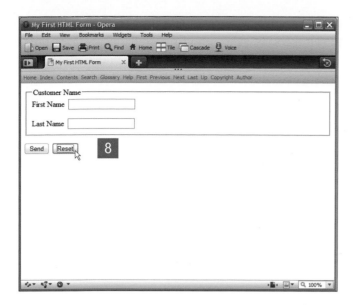

7 Add two non-breaking spaces (` `). Add another `<button>` element with the `type` attribute set to `"reset"` and the text content between the tags as 'Reset'.

8 Save the HTML file and load it in your web browser to view the results. Fill in the 'First Name' and 'Last Name' fields and click the 'Send' button. An e-mail with a preformatted subject line will appear. If you go back to the form and click the Reset button, the form will be cleared.

Adding a selection box to an HTML form

Many web forms allow users to select from a list of items in a dropdown menu or selection box. Depending on their purpose, they may allow users to select more than one item from the list. Adding selection boxes to an HTML form is a fast and easy way to provide users with both a choice of selections and limit their selections to a set list.

Table 7.4 Tags used in this task

Tag	Function
`<select>`… `</select>`	Specifies a selection list or dropdown menu box. The **size** attribute specifies how many list items to display.
`<option>`… `</option>`	Provides a list of options for various HTML controls.
`<optgroup>`… `</optgroup>`	Groups a series of options together that are presented in a user interface, under a common label.

The `<select>` element specifies the use of a select list control. The **size** attribute specifies how many options from the list to display to users – it must be an integer greater than zero. The **multiple** attribute allows users to select more than one item from the list.

Important

The **multiple** attribute is a Boolean one. Its presence signifies the attribute is on, while its absence signifies it is off. When using the **multiple** attribute, simply putting the keyword into the start tag enables multiple selections to be made from the list, while leaving it out keeps this feature off. Unlike other attribute values, the **multiple** attribute is *not* enclosed in double quotes.

The `<option>` element provides the list of options from which users will choose. An `<optgroup>` element can be used to group a series of `<option>` elements together under a common label displayed in the dropdown menu or list. The label displayed is set in the `label` attribute, which is enclosed in double quotes.

Ideally, the options will have values which can be sent to the web server to be processed in some way. Capturing data is not a capability of the HTML form itself, however – it must be done with other scripting or programming languages.

In this task, you will add a `<select>` control to an HTML form and specify multiple selections. You will also provide `<optgroup>` labels for, and `<option>` element list

Adding a selection box to an HTML form (cont.)

7

1 Open your HTML template in your text editor and save it with a new name. Alternatively, you can use the form you created in the previous task and remove all the controls from the `<form>` element.

2 In the `<body>` element, add a `<form>` element if it isn't there. Add the `post` method attribute and the `enctype="plain/text"` attribute to the start tag.

3 In the `<form>` element, add a `<select>` element. Do not add the `multiple` attribute.

4 In the `<select>` element, add three `<optgroup>` elements and provide the following values for the `label` attributes: **"Primary"**, **"Secondary"** and **"Tertiary"**, respectively.

Adding a selection box to an HTML form (cont.)

items to, the list in order to give users options from which to choose. Note that the optional end tags for the `<optgroup>` and `<option>` elements have been left out in my example HTML files. Again, it's never a bad practice to include them, but they are optional.

5 In each of the `<optgroup>` elements, add three `<option>` elements. In the 'Primary' `<optgroup>` element, list 'Red', 'Blue' and 'Yellow'. In the 'Secondary' `<optgroup>` element, list 'Orange', 'Violet' and 'Green'. In the 'Tertiary' `<optgroup>` list 'Red-Orange', 'Blue-Violet' and 'Yellow-Green'. Set unique **value** attributes for them if you like.

6 Add a `<label>` element to enclose the `<select>` element. Use the text content 'Colors', followed by two non-breaking space special characters. Place the end tag below the `</select>` end tag.

7 Save the HTML file and open it in your web browser.

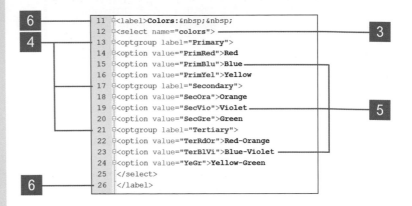

```
11  <label>Colors:  
12  <select name="colors">
13  <optgroup label="Primary">
14  <option value="PrimRed">Red
15  <option value="PrimBlu">Blue
16  <option value="PrimYel">Yellow
17  <optgroup label="Secondary">
18  <option value="SecOra">Orange
19  <option value="SecVio">Violet
20  <option value="SecGre">Green
21  <optgroup label="Tertiary">
22  <option value="TerRdOr">Red-Orange
23  <option value="TerBlVi">Blue-Violet
24  <option value="YeGr">Yellow-Green
25  </select>
26  </label>
```

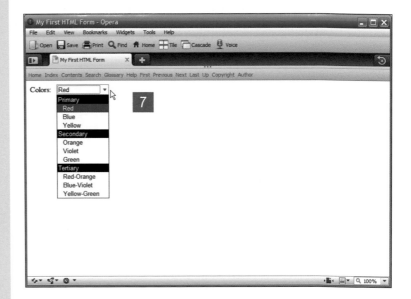

The `<input />` element in HTML wears many different faces. In HTML5, there are more than a dozen *new* faces the element can wear. The good news is that it is backward compatibile, thank goodness! That means nothing built with older versions of HTML will break going forwards. The bad news, however, is there are more than a dozen new `<input>` controls to learn.

The final piece of good news, though, is they're very cool controls and make for much nicer, more user-friendly web forms.

7

Table 7.5 Tag used in this task

Tag	Function
`<input />`	Specifies an HTML control. The **type** attribute can be set to indicate the type of control to use. HTML5 specifications definc the following new types of input controls:
	`email`
	`tel`
	`url`
	`number`
	`range`
	`date`
	`month`
	`week`
	`time`
	`datetime`
	`datetime-local`
	`search`
	`color`

Browsers do not all understand how to interpret the new `<input />` type definitions. In the event a browser doesn't recognise the type attribute, it will simply display the control as a text box – a default fall-back position. This ensures all browsers will handle the controls of an HTML5 form without errors and unexpected results, even if the browser is a legacy version.

Jargon buster

Legacy – Older versions of software or hardware which must be accounted for in web design. An example of a legacy browser is Internet Explorer 6.0, which is still in use at the time of writing in some organisations.

Using HTML `<input />` controls (cont.)

The `type` attribute causes browsers to handle the input in different ways. For example, in some versions, a browser will not display the e-mail type any differently from a normal text box, but the Apple iPhone provides users with an e-mail address-specific touchscreen keyboard when it encounters an e-mail-type `<input />` control. This behaviour will become more and more prevalent in newer, more modern browsers and smartphone devices, though specifications may be implemented differently.

i

For your information

If you have not upgraded your web browser for some time or if the one you're using isn't compliant with a particular standard in its current version, you may not be able to view the results of all the tasks which follow. Not all browsers support all HTML5 specifications and recommendations yet. In the screenshots for this book, I've used several different web browsers, but primarily Opera™. In some of the screenshots you will see in this chapter, Safari (for Windows) has been used to show the results. If you cannot see your own results for a particular task, using another web browser might help.

In this task, you will add several `<input />` controls to a web form and assign them different HTML5 `type` attributes. In your web browser, the results can be seen in some cases and in others they are not going to be visible. In subsequent chapters, we'll work with the controls we create here.

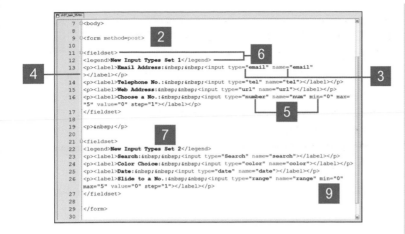

7

1. Open your HTML template in your text editor and save it with a new name or use the web form you created in the previous task.

2. Add the **method=post** attribute to the **<form>** element start tag if it's not already there.

3. Add four **<input />** tags and set the **type** attribute for each as follows: **"email"**, **"tel"**, **"url"** and **"number"**. Give them each a **name** attribute which matches the **type** attribute.

4. Place a **<p>** element and add a **<label>** element with the control's name around each control.

5. In the number **<input />** control, add the attributes **min="0"**, **max="5"** and **step="1"** before the trailing forward slash.

6. Enclose the **<input />** controls in a **<fieldset>** element and add a **<legend>** element before the first **<input />** control with the text content 'New Input Types Set 1'.

Important

The **type="number"** **<input />** control is a spinbox or a number box which allows users to select a number from a range of numbers by using an increase (up) or decrease (down) arrow. Spinboxes are used, in general, to select quantities and the numbers are integers.

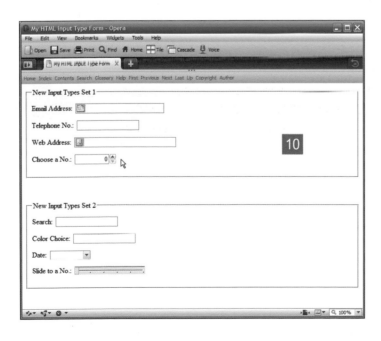

Using HTML
`<input />`
controls (cont.)

7 Repeat steps 2–6, this time labelling the `<fieldset>` with the `<legend>` content 'New Input Types Set 2' and add four more `<input />` controls.

8 Add the `type` attribute to each control with the values `"search"`, `"color"` (note the US spelling!), `"date"` and `"range"`, respectively.

9 In the 'range' control tag, add the attributes `min="0"`, `max="5"`, `value="0"` and `step="1"`.

10 Save your HTML file and open it in your web browser to view the finished form.

Timesaver tip

You can copy and paste the existing `<input />` elements and simply edit the `type` attributes in each. Remember, copy and paste is your friend when doing repetitive markup.

Important

This is by no means an exhaustive list of the states available for the `type` attribute of the `<input />` element, but these types are specifically new to HTML5. Check the online documentation for a complete list of currently available types (at: **www.whatwg.org**).

For your information

The `type="date"` control showed up on your web page as a plain text box, with no controls anywhere on it, didn't it? Yeah, I thought so. If it didn't, you're using the Opera™ browser and you're using a version later than version 9.0. Opera 9.0™ and later is the only browser around right now which supports the `type="date"` control at the time of writing.

You probably also noticed that your `type="color"` control is just a text box, too. It's a shame, but at the time of writing, no browser supports that functionality yet. Finally, you probably saw that your Search box looked and acted just like a text box too. It's disappointing, but if you are using a Mac with Safari, you saw the Search box with rounded corners. When you type in it, a little 'x' appears at the far right of the box, which will clear the Search box if you click it. So, even though a few of these new types don't work yet, you still get a clear idea of how interesting and exciting HTML will be when these control types and many others are supported by most or all browsers.

Adding more HTML form controls

It should be clear by now that the `<input />` element is a very important one for HTML controls. There are so many different types of controls which use it as their primary markup it isn't possible to cover them exhaustively here. A few of the more common ones, however, are used in this task so you can familiarise yourself with the most basic and commonly used HTML controls.

Table 7.6 Tags used in this task

Tag	Function
`<input />`	Specifies an HTML control, with the following `type` attributes determining the type of control: `checkbox` `radio` `password` `file`
`<textarea>...` `</textarea>`	Specifies a text area field – a field capable of holding far more text data than a `text` type field.

The `<textarea>` element provides a large input area for text data. You will have seen examples on many websites, especially if you've ever posted a CV or applied for a job online.

A text area is a multiline plain text entry area, like an online version of Notepad. If the text area is made read-only, it can be used to present disclaimers and end user licence agreements (EULAs) within a specified region of the page, rather than users having to open an additional page or taking up a large section of the page with the information. It can also be made editable to provide a place for more detailed input than the usual text field allows.

The `<textarea>` element allows control over how many characters to allow per line by means of the `cols` attribute, set to a number other than zero. It determines how many lines to present onscreen using the `rows` attribute. You can limit the amount of data in the `<textarea>` element with the `maxlength` attribute.

Tick boxes (or checkboxes) are among the most common controls used. They allow users to mark selections from a list or group of choices where more than one is appropriate (such as a 'Tick all that apply' area of a form). Tick boxes are generally square in appearance on the screen and are created using the `<input />` element with a `type` attribute of `checkbox`.

Radio buttons, or option buttons, are on or off, clickable controls which only permit one selection to be made from a group of available choices. Unlike tick boxes, radio buttons are not used alone but when a choice is required, such as 'Yes' or 'No' in sections of licence agreements.

Radio buttons are often grouped together in an option group to make the choices clear for users. Radio buttons are created using the `<input />` element, setting the `type` attribute to `radio`.

A password field is a text field which obscures an entry as a user types. It replaces the text with either asterisks (*) or bullet points. The aim is to offer security and it's used almost everywhere on the Internet. Anywhere a login is required, the password field will be seen. It's created using an `<input />` element and `type` attribute `password`.

A file picker is a special field which opens a dialogue box to browse for and select a file to upload from the local computer. This field is frequently seen on the Internet also, wherever a file is stored on a web server from the local machine. The `<input />` element's `type` attribute is set to `file` to create the file picker.

! Important

There are many other attributes and associated settings required with `<textarea>` elements. These are detailed in the WHATWG's online documentation (at: **www.whatwg.org**).

i For your information

This section by no means represents a comprehensive covering of the WHATWG's recommendations for HTML controls. There are many attributes, values and settings which can be used to great effect by web developers and programmers. This section just gives you a taste so that you can be inspired to go away and learn more.

Adding more HTML form controls (cont.)

This task will enable you to add a few more controls to your repertoire of HTML form objects. When you view the results in your browser, it will become clear how the browser interprets the HTML markup for each one. The password field is a text field which hides the text being entered, while the file picker provides a button to click so the file selection dialogue box appears. Radio buttons, tick boxes, password fields and file pickers are all extremely common on web forms, so knowing how to create and configure them is essential.

1 Open the sample web page you made in the previous task in your text editor and save it with a new name.

2 Below the second `<fieldset>` element, add an empty paragraph element.

3 Under the `<p>` element, add a new `<fieldset>` element with a `<legend>` element containing the text 'Common Input Types'.

4 Within the `<fieldset>` element, add a `<p>` element and a second `<fieldset>` element with a `<legend>` element containing the text 'Checkbox array'.

5 In the nested `<fieldset>`, add three `<input />` controls and set the `type` attribute to `"checkbox"` for all of them. Include a label for each one, naming them 'Checkbox 1', 'Checkbox 2' and 'Checkbox 3', respectively. You may also include the name attribute for the `<input />` controls if you want, matching the name to the label for each.

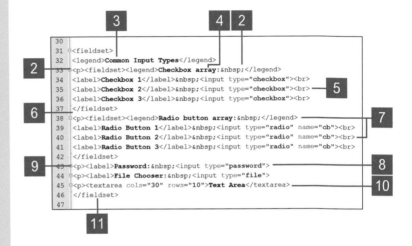

For your information

An 'empty' paragraph actually isn't. It should contain the special character for a non-breaking space (` `).

For your information

Placing one element inside another element of the same type is called 'nesting'.

136

Timesaver tip

It's much faster – and I do mean *much* faster – to copy and paste the checkbox array and simply change the 'checkbox' references to 'radio' for the `type` attribute and 'Radio button' in all `<label>` and `<legend>` elements. You will have this part of the task done in a fraction of the time of typing it all from scratch if you utilise copy and paste.

Important

A web browser knows any radio buttons with the same name are mutually exclusive – that is, only one of them can be active or clicked. Clicking one automatically clears the others of the same name.

Important

Note that both a start and an end tag are required for a `<textarea>` element. Any text content between the tags is used as initial text in the field. This is *not* the same as placeholder text, however, which is what appears in a field until a user enters the field.

Adding more HTML form controls (cont.)

7

6 Close the `<fieldset>` element and add another empty `<p>` element.

7 Beneath the paragraph element, repeat steps 3 to 6, changing the `checkbox` type to `radio` in all `<input />` elements and adjusting the labels and any name attributes to radio buttons instead of checkboxes. Ensure the `<legend>` says 'Radio button array' instead of 'Checkbox array'. This time, name each of the controls the *same*, such as `"radio"`.

8 Below the radio buttons, add another paragraph element and an `<input />` element of `type "password"`.

9 Below the password field, add another `<p>` element and add an `<input />` control of `type "file"`.

10 Finally, add another `<p>` element beneath the file picker control and add the `<textarea>` element. Set the `cols` attribute to 30 and the `rows` attribute to 10.

Adding more HTML form controls (cont.)

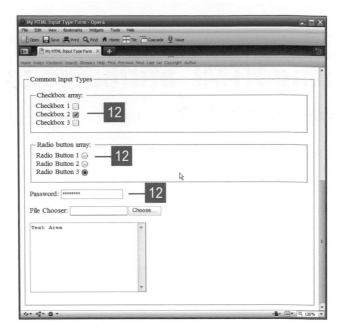

11 Close the `<fieldset>` element and ensure all the preceding `<fieldsets>` are properly closed, too.

12 Save the HTML file and view it in your web browser to see the results. Type an entry in the password field, enter some text in the text area and select some of the radio buttons and tick boxes to ensure they all function correctly.

Using HTML attributes to tweak forms

Introduction

So far, you've learned how to structure an HTML page, create and set out tables, mark up text and do all sorts of fun HTML things. HTML can do so much more, though, and the future of HTML is exciting and fun.

The good news is, HTML5 is going to be a powerful markup language – and perhaps the best markup language variation ever produced. The bad news is, lots of proposed changes don't work at this time and a lot of the exciting 'bells and whistles' HTML5 is able to provide don't come natively in HTML, but work in conjunction with other web languages, such as JavaScript. HTML5 is powerful, though, and can provide new avenues of creativity which are impossible without the use of programming and scripting. Unfortunately, many of those things still require programming and scripting … which, sadly, are well outside the scope of this book.

All the same, we can still discuss a few things, so long as it is understood we look at these things from a strictly HTML standpoint. A high-level overview of one such aspect of HTML5, video, provides the ability to embed a video natively into an HTML5 page and doesn't require a third-party player to run. There are a lot of factors on which that small feat relies, however, and one of them is whether or not the video is in the right format and the browser displaying the page is the right version (most modern browsers are fine).

What you'll do

Add placeholder text in HTML form controls

Set a field to autofocus

Find out what *doesn't* work

HTML5 is more than just a new set of tags, though. It's also a new set of attributes which can be used to assist with making the web page a new experience. These new attributes have many applications, but HTML forms make good use of them, so we'll discuss a few of them in relation to how they make forms better, clearer and more accessible than ever before.

In addition, HTML5 isn't just new tags – it recommends the obsolescence of some tags, too. That's a fancy way of saying some tags are no longer supported in HTML5, which in turn means most modern browsers (without backwards compatibility for those tags) won't register them either. Those tags will be ignored and have no effect on content. This chapter provides a list of those deprecated tags, though it should not be considered exhaustive.

Finally, as the book has unfurled, you have created an HTML template and a couple of sample web pages to enable you to practise using new elements and tags. In this chapter we will 'clean up' one of those templates and create a clean, uncluttered sample web page to use as we move forward to Cascading Style Sheets (CSS) in the next chapter. This will provide you with markup practice, an opportunity to refresh your memory of earlier chapters if you need to, give you practise in reading and picking through markup and eventually give you a suitable page to use for future tasks.

HTML, as you know, consists of elements composed of tags and most also have attributes, the values of which specify certain aspects of the tags' functions or appearance. For example, the `<img />` tag uses the `src` attribute to specify which picture to show. The `<a>` element uses the `href` attribute to specify the anchor point for the hyperlink.

One of HTML5's new features is the `placeholder` attribute, which specifies placeholder text to put into an HTML form field. This had to be done in other ways in previous HTML versions, but HTML5 form controls which may need it, such as text boxes, e-mail address fields or URL fields, can contain placeholder text to improve the user interface.

Of course, as is the case with any HTML element or attribute, support for their functionality isn't universal, by any stretch of the imagination. The `placeholder` attribute is functional in the Safari browser for versions 4.0 or later, Google Chrome's browser, versions 4.0 and greater, the Firefox browser, versions 3.7 and later and iPhone 4.0 handheld devices and newer, at least, at the time of writing. The screenshot provided for this task is from Safari 5.0 for Windows.

As you can see, this task doesn't have an accompanying table listing the tags used, as we have had so far. This is because there are many tags which can take the `placeholder` attribute. In the task we will focus on three – the text, URL and e-mail fields, which were also discussed in the previous chapter.

The results of this task provide placeholder text for the fields on your sample page, to which we will add the placeholder attribute. You will specify the type of data the field should contain so that, even if the user's browser doesn't display the form control correctly, the interface will not become confusing or unclear.

Adding placeholder text in HTML form controls

8

Cross reference

See Chapter 7 for more details about HTML form elements.

Adding placeholder text in HTML form controls (cont.)

```
11  <fieldset>
12  <legend>New Input Types Set 1</legend>
13  <p><label>Email Address:  <input type="email" name="email"
    placeholder="Enter email address here"></label></p>
14  <p><label>Telephone No.:  <input type="tel" name="tel"
    ></label></p>
15  <p><label>Web Address:  <input type="url" name="url"
    placeholder="Enter web address here"></label></p>
16  <p><label>Choose a No.:  <input type="number" name="num"
    min="0" max="5" value="0" step="1"></label></p>
17  </fieldset>
```

1. In your text editor, open the sample HTML form you created in Chapter 7 and save it with a new name.

2. Locate the `<input />` element of type `email`.

3. In the start tag, add the placeholder element with the value 'Enter email address here'.

4. Locate the `<input />` element of type `url` and add the `placeholder` attribute with the value 'Enter web address here'.

5. Save the HTML file and open it in your browser.

Important

Again, not all browsers support the `placeholder` attribute functionality. So, if you can't see the placeholder text, try downloading a newer version of your browser. If you still can't see it, try downloading Safari, if you're able to do so with your operating system. It's sure to work on that one!

HTML markup previously didn't offer web form designers any way to set the focus of a particular field on opening a web page. To set the focus on a particular field as the page loaded, web developers and designers resorted to scripting languages. That meant pages might partially load before the script executed and moved the cursor or power users and the visually disabled might mistakenly type in the wrong field when the script set the focus, not to mention the potential security risks.

Setting the focus for a form can be important if the order in which information is entered is critical. Using HTML5 rather than a script to set focus has the advantage of giving you control over when the focus is set and gives browser vendors and browser extension programmers an opportunity to disable the functionality when it would be inconvenient, since there is no JavaScript (or any other scripting language) which has to be bypassed or ignored.

Focus is set using the `autofocus` attribute of HTML form controls. All HTML5 form controls utilise the `autofocus` attribute. This allows form designers and developers to use any type of control desired as the autofocus control (as opposed to *having* to use a text field, for instance). Using `autofocus` enables HTML applications which are intuitive, fast, easy to navigate and learn.

The `autofocus` attribute is not a valued attribute. That is, it requires no value in double quotes to be entered to set it. It's a Boolean attribute – its presence in the element enables it for that control while its absence disables it.

In this task, you will apply the `autofocus` attribute to a control on the sample web form you made in the previous task. When the page loads, the cursor will be placed in the appropriate field automatically.

Setting a field to autofocus

8

Setting a field to autofocus (cont.)

```
21  <fieldset>
22  <legend>New Input Types Set 2</legend>
23  <p><label>Search:  <input type="Search" name="search"
    autofocus></label></p>
24  <p><label>Color Choice:  <input type="color" name="color"
    ></label></p>
25  <p><label>Date:  <input type="date" name="date"
    ></label></p>
26  <p><label>Slide to a No.:  <input type="range" name=
    "range" min="0" max="5" value="0" step="1"></label></p>
27  </fieldset>
```

1 Open the web form you created in the previous task in your text editor and save it with a new name.

2 Locate the search field on the form.

3 In the start tag, add the `autofocus` attribute. Remember the autofocus attribute is Boolean, and doesn't require a value to be set.

4 Save the HTML file and, when you open it in your web browser, the cursor will be placed in the search box.

For your information

As technology changes, HTML adapts to accommodate the changes. For example, one of the advantages of HTML5 is how the elements work for handheld devices. The iPhone, for example, will place a special keyboard onscreen with a small space bar and a prominent '@' symbol to make entering e-mail addresses easier when it encounters an `email <input />` element on a web page. E-mail addresses do not have spaces as a general rule, but almost all of them have the '@' symbol in them. The iPhone also customises the keyboard for a `url <input />` element, providing a prominent 'dot' key rather than the one on a standard keyboard.

As you can see, this section isn't a task. Rather, it provides a list of elements which *aren't* supported by HTML5. Browsers which comply with the new specification may or may not support legacy elements and tags, but, be assured, future versions of browsers definitely *won't* support them.

If you've tried to mark up text on a web page for some reason – commenting on a blog post, for instance, or on a news article – and found one of the tags didn't work, it may well be your browser has been updated and stopped supporting that element or tag. (This has happened to me. When it occurs, the browser ignores the tag and simply renders the content as normal text. That can be very embarrassing.)

The list in Table 8.1 shouldn't be considered an exhaustive list. You can always check the WHATWG's online documentation for the latest HTML specification, as well as the W3C's site. While the WHATWG has the latest such details and recommendations, the W3C updates its site as well. Between the two, you're sure to find what you're looking for.

What *doesn't* work

8

What *doesn't* work (cont.)

Table 8.1 Deprecated HTML tags

Tags (elements)	Description
`<acronym>`	Defines an acronym.
`<applet>`	Defines an applet.
`<basefont>`	Defines a base font for the page.
`<big>`	Defines big text.
`<center>`	Defines centred text.
`<dir>`	Defines a directory list.
`<font>`	Defines text font, size and colour.
`<frame>`	Defines a frame.
`<frameset>`	Defines a set of frames.
`<isindex>`	Defines a single-line input field.
`<noframes>`	Defines a noframe section.
`<s>`	Defines strikethrough (crossed out) text.
`<strike>`	Defines strikethrough text.
`<tt>`	Defines teletype text.
`<u>`	Defines underlined text.

CSS3 – what's new?

Introduction

CSS, like HTML, exists in different versions which have evolved over time. Up to CSS2, the entire document recommendation for CSS was submitted to the W3C all at once, as a single block of information. That meant the process of getting the recommendations approved and then implemented via browser manufacturers took a long time.

One of the new things about CSS3 is that it's not being submitted in its entirety as a single recommendation, but split into separate modules which are independently submitted and approved. The recommendations can thus be implemented faster by browser vendors, and designers can use the new features faster.

Aside from how the specification is submitted, there are new things which create formatting options previously unavailable. CSS3 provides ways to format web pages not possible before without the help of programming or scripting languages.

What you'll do

Find documentation on CSS

Find out what's new in CSS3

Finding documentation on CSS

Information about CSS3 isn't hard to find. An Internet search using any search engine will produce huge numbers of pages related to CSS3. Much of the information will be redundant or less than useful, but a few sites stand out as giving valuable information.

First and foremost is the W3C itself. It maintains a document on its website which is updated when major recommendation changes are made (visit **www.w3.org** and follow its CSS links to find the latest specification documentation).

In addition, a helpful quick reference guide (QRG) can be downloaded free of charge at **www.veign.com**. It is an extremely helpful guide as it lists the CSS properties alongside their value settings, as well as pseudo-classes, measurement units used in CSS, and selectors with examples to choose any matching (or all) selectors. It's a very complete resource and I highly recommend it.

For your information

Don't be too concerned if the terms like 'pseudo-classes' and 'selectors' don't seem to make much sense right now. They'll be covered in more detail as the book progresses and, where necessary, definitions will be provided.

In this task, we will collect materials for use with the HTML template we created and will be referencing CSS properties and value settings from several of the sources you've gathered.

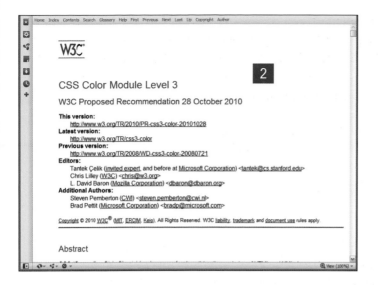

1 Open your web browser and navigate to **www.w3.org**.

2 Locate the information about CSS3 on the website.

3 Bookmark the W3C specification for CSS in your browser.

Important

The W3C updates its website and the location of the specific document for CSS3's specification may change from time to time. Be sure to examine the site carefully when you visit to ensure you have the latest information about CSS3 and not an earlier version.

Timesaver tip

You probably already have the W3C website bookmarked. If not, do so now. It can save you a lot of time searching the Internet later. You can find a lot of timely, helpful information there on CSS3 and HTML5, so it's one of your primary sources. Be sure to check the site out thoroughly, along with the WHATWG site at **www.whatwg.org**.

9

Finding documentation on CSS (cont.)

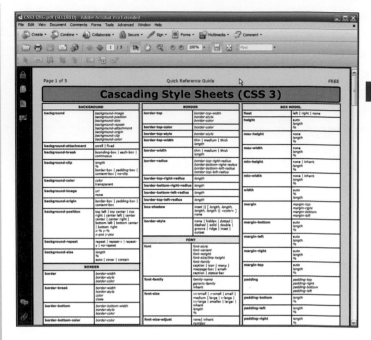

4 Navigate to **www.veign.com** using your web browser. If you have not done so already, download the CSS3 quick reference guide (QRG) you will find there.

One of the key things about technology is how rapidly it changes. Fortunately, there are people and organisations dedicated to keeping up with these changes and making sense of it all. They also present the information in helpful, easy-to-understand formats so anyone can check up on what's new and exciting in a single sitting and understand it without much trouble.

One such website is CSS3.info (**www.css3.info**). There you will find a terrific amount of up-to-date information about CSS which will prove invaluable to you as a CSS developer.

For your information

CSS3.info is one of the best blogs on the Internet for keeping track of what's happening with CSS3 and should be among the first, if not *the* first, stops you make when seeking CSS3-specific online information.

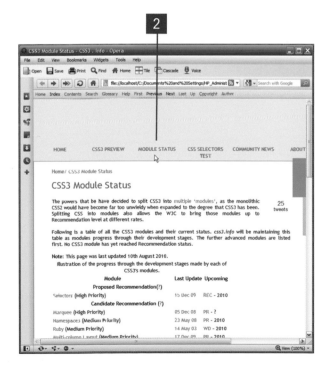

1 Open your web browser and navigate to **www.css3.info**.

2 Click on the Module status tab at the top of the screen.

3 Note the latest updates and the status of all the modules being put through the approval process.

4 Bookmark the tab in your browser and return to it from time to time to check for any new information or updates.

Important

Perusing information on a website may seem like a frivolous step on which to build an entire task, but it really isn't. It's a critical part of learning to use and understand CSS and its components properly. You can't use something effectively if you don't know about it, so bookmarking pages which tell you about what's new and ready is important.

9

Introduction to CSS

Introduction

If you've worked through the tasks in this book sequentially, you will have seen references made to CSS several times and even used it a few times along the way. CSS stands for Cascading Style Sheets and, while HTML provides the structure for web pages, CSS controls their appearance.

CSS are text documents which contain formatting instructions for browsers about specific elements, sections or pages of websites. The instructions apply to all elements covered by the instruction set, no matter where they appear on the web page. CSS 'cascades' in that the instructions for one layer are overridden by the next layer down. Formatting, therefore, cascades downwards in priority. If that seems a little confusing, bear with me and it will become clearer.

CSS format a website on three different levels. In general, only one level is chosen for each page. The first level is an external style sheet, a separate text document which exists as its own file on the web server and to which the HTML file(s) using it refers. This provides overall formatting instructions for all pages which refer to it. The second level places the formatting (or style) instructions in the `<style>` element of the HTML file's `<head>` section. This level of cascade operates only for the page on which the style is included and overrides instructions from the external style sheet if they should conflict. The third cascade level is an inline style. Inline styles are included in the `style` attribute of the start tag for the element it formats. This is the lowest cascade level and it overrides both levels above it.

What you'll do

Prep for CSS

Understand CSS code

Create CSS comments

Understand classes and IDs

Style sheets cascade down rather than up because the browser interprets the formatting instructions in that order. First, the browser checks the HTML file and if an external style sheet reference exists, it applies the formatting there. If the browser then locates a `<style>` element in the `<head>` of the document, it applies those styles, overriding the styles from the external style sheet. Finally, the browser interprets individual tags in the `<body>` element and applies style attributes from the individual elements, overriding any previous styles.

Many of the formatting responsibilities of previous versions of HTML have been moved to CSS instead. Style sheets define formatting with greater efficiency and precision and offer a single location for all (or at least most) formatting instructions. This offers distinct advantages in terms of application and troubleshooting. When new pages are added to a site or if content on an existing page changes, the formatting for the page is automatically applied as soon as the page goes live. If something hasn't been formatted correctly, it can be changed in a central location rather than on each page or even every section of each page.

CSS3 differs in a couple of major ways from CSS2 or CSS2.01, the previous incarnations, but the most significant change is in how the specifications are proposed and made available for browser vendors. Rather than compiling the entire specification for approval, CSS3 is offered in modules. The modules provide a faster, easier way to access the recommendations via the W3C and load them on modern browsers. Other significant changes include greater flexibility for borders and backgrounds, content columns, and greater paged media support for print. As the other modules for CSS3 continue to make their way through the W3C, how web pages are formatted and CSS is used and web-based print is formatted is exciting.

Having an HTML template to use for CSS code is helpful and will save us having to do the markup as we go along in addition to the CSS coding. To make things easier, we'll take this opportunity to clean up one of our previous HTML templates so we can use it for our CSS tasks to come.

We'll make use of one of the completed HTML templates from a sample page we created earlier in the book and remove all the spurious markup elements so we only have the structure and content portions. Once that's completed we'll save it with a new template name. Make sure it's something you can recall easily because we'll be using that template for the remainder of the book.

Also remember the tasks build on one another. If you skip any of the tasks along the way, you may then need to adjust the code to accommodate your particular template.

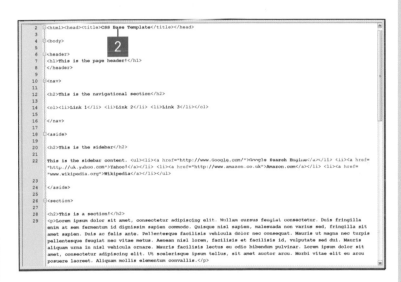

1 Using your text editor, open the file for the first task you completed in Chapter 4. This will be your HTML template we will 'clean up' for use in subsequent tasks throughout the book. Save the template with a new name.

2 In the `<title>` element, change the content to 'CSS Base Template'.

3 Locate and remove any `style=` codes from any of the start tags throughout the entire template.

i

For your information

If you're unsure what HTML you should use from Chapter 4, refer back to Chapter 3's final task and progress forwards from there. Alternatively, all you need is a basic HTML page structure with all the HTML5 structural elements in place. If you know what the markup is to create it from scratch, you can just make your own.

10

Prepping for CSS (cont.)

4 Remove all HTML font formatting markup elements (such as `<var>`, `<code>`, `<em>`, `<blockquote>` elements), *except* the heading elements (`<h1>` elements, `<h2>` elements and so on), from all sections of the template.

5 Save the HTML file when you've finished and view it in your web browser to ensure everything looks as it should. You should not have any links in the `<nav>` element at this time, but the external links in the `<aside>` element should have been retained. (It is not critical for the rest of the book for them to be there, however.)

Timesaver tip

Use the search feature in your text editor to accomplish step 3 quickly and easily. Simply enter 'style=' in the search box and click **Find** to be shown all the instances on the page in turn. Remove the attribute from all tags (along with its value, of course) manually to avoid mistakes.

In Chapter 1, we discussed HTML's element structure and how the various pieces fit together to form HTML markup code overall. CSS is similar. There are pieces which make up CSS' code syntax, so understanding what those pieces are helps us understand the whole and put together effective CSS code.

CSS code is composed of several discrete components which form its rules or instructions. The selector declares which element the formatting will apply to, the property declares what part of the element is formatted and the value states what formatting is being applied to the element.

Selector – declares which element is being formatted.

Property – declares which aspect of the element is being formatted.

Value – the formatting which is being applied.

As you can see above, the element selector is the first part of the CSS code. On the same line, beside the element, is an opening curly bracket ({), followed by the property declarations and, after a colon, the values for them. The rule is closed with a closing curly bracket (}).

Several formatting properties can be applied to an element in a single declaration, rather than it being necessary to type a rule for each property. When declaring multiple rules for a single element, each property declaration is separated from its value by a colon, then a semicolon separates each property declaration from the next inside the curly brackets.

It is also possible to declare the same rule for more than one element in a similar way. In such cases, all the selectors to which the rule is to be applied are listed before the curly brackets, separated by commas, thus:

```
aside, nav {background:palegreen;
font-size: 10px}
```

Understanding CSS code

Jargon buster

Syntax – The rules for the appropriate use of components, whether computer or linguistic in nature, so a cohesive language and grammatical structure are formed. How components of a language of any kind are used to create the proper elements of the language.

10

Understanding CSS code (cont.)

Style sheets, particularly external ones, can be quite lengthy. Most very attractive websites use incredibly intricate style sheets to control formatting and provide a uniform appearance for the site (examples of extensive CSS are available at: **www.freecsstemplates.org,** where you can download a free template). Open the source code on your web browser and examine the code. This will help you become familiar with what external style sheets look like and how they're laid out.

In this task, we will apply a simple `<style>` element style sheet to the paragraph elements on our sample web page to change their font colour.

1 Navigate to **www.freecsstemplates.org** with your web browser.

2 Select a CSS template you like from the selection of free templates and download it on to your computer. You can use the Yosemite one like me if you wish.

3 Open the index.html web page in a web browser to review the appearance of the page.

4 Open the style sheet – called style.css – in your text editor and review the rules. Be sure you're able to identify the rule components: Selectors, properties and values.

```
1
2    /*
3    Design by Free CSS Templates  I
4    http://www.freecsstemplates.org
5    Released for free under a Creative Commons Attribution 2.5 License
6    */
7
8    body {
9        margin: 0;
10       padding: 0;
11       background: #F1F1F1 url(images/img01.gif) repeat-x left top;
12       font-family: Arial, Helvetica, sans-serif;
13       font-size: 12px;
14       color: #787878;
15   }
16
17   h1, h2, h3 {
18       margin: 0;
19       padding: 0;
20       font-weight: normal;
21       color: #023848;
22   }
23
24   h1 {
25       font-size: 2em;
26   }
27
```

Creating CSS comments

1 Open the folder for the CSS template you downloaded in the previous task.

2 Find the style.css file in the folder.

3 Open the style.css file in your text editor.

4 At the top of the text file, notice the /* comment indicator and the */ indicator at the end of the comment. These are the start and end tags for a CSS comment.

5 Note the other CSS comments annotating the rest of the style.css file.

Just as with HTML, it may be necessary to annotate the CSS code you write. To annotate code, use CSS comments. They work the same way as do comments in other programming or markup languages – they are ignored by the browser, which does not display or interpret them, but they're visible to programmers working behind the scenes.

Comments are used to explain the code, make notes regarding the code itself and as reminders to the programmer to do various tasks. Comments in CSS are enclosed between two forward slashes and two asterisks (/*...*/). Like HTML comments, CSS comments are completely ignored by the browser.

In this task you will see the CSS comments in a style sheet with the browser by viewing the page source. Notice the comment will be visible only in the page source.

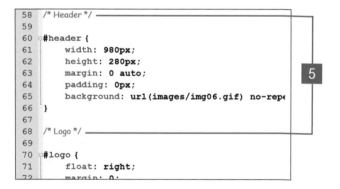

For your information

If you use Notepad++ or a similar text editor, the comments for all code are indicated by coloured text. In Notepad++ the default colour is green. This is a helpful feature when you are reading code.

CSS selectors are used to pick an element for formatting and the formatting is then applied to all instances of that element. For example, if you create a rule for the paragraph element (`<p>`), the rule you create is applied to all `<p>` elements on the page or the site (depending on where the CSS is in the cascading levels). What, though, if you only want to format a single paragraph for a certain instance?

Well, one way to do this is to use inline styles, but, if you have several properties to format, you'll want to use a style sheet to pick out the element and format those properties. Doing this will help keep your code clean and easy to manage. How, though, can you single out a particular paragraph in this way? Harder still, how can a particular group of `<p>` be chosen from among all the other `<p>` elements in the site in order to apply specific formatting to it alone?

Enter HTML classes to the rescue! To utilise CSS more fully, we must revert to our HTML code and invoke the `class` and `id` attributes. Every HTML element has `class` and `id` attributes which can be set so formatting with CSS (and other useful functions, too) can be performed easily and for only a select group of elements.

Classes simply group HTML elements together. Specific element property formatting can then be applied only to the elements of the chosen class.

Lumping elements into a class is fine, but if one element of a certain type needs different formatting, it can be identified individually from among other elements or a class of elements by means of its `id` attribute. Think of the `id` attribute as a way to make an individual element stand out amid other elements of the same type. It's a way to single it out for special treatment, such as individually formatting a single paragraph in other text content.

Understanding classes and IDs

10

Understanding classes and IDs (cont.)

Important

An `id` for an element is analogous to a name for it. You can create rules for individual elements among the other elements and `class` attributes by specifying its name in the rule(s).

1 Open the folder for the CSS template you downloaded in the second task in this chapter.

2 Open the index.htm file in your text editor (not your web browser!).

3 Observe the `<div>` elements in this template. This template is not based on HTML5, but on an earlier version of HTML. The structural elements didn't exist as they do with HTML5. Therefore, generic `<div>` elements have been created as 'wrappers' for content and CSS formatting can be applied to them.

4 Note the extensive use of the `class` and `id` attributes throughout the web page. Almost all the elements have either a `class` or `id` attribute set.

In this task, you will observe the use of the `class` attribute with the `<div>` element from an older CSS template. By specifying the `class`, certain formatting can be applied to each member of the `class` at the same time, rather than having to do it individually or to all the elements of the same type indiscriminately.

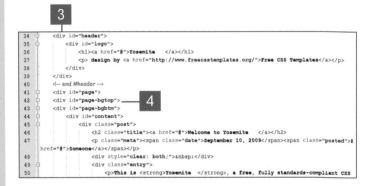

Important

Maybe you did not download an HTML5 template from the website provided. You may, however, find other HTML5 CSS templates on the Internet. It's important to note that this task assumes you did not locate an HTML5-specific template.

Specifying CSS styles

Introduction

So far, a lot of the CSS work covered has involved observing and gathering information and materials. Now it's time to start coding some CSS, to get our hands 'dirty', as it were! That involves learning about how to create a style sheet from the ground up.

Cascading Style Sheets are text documents, nothing more. They have the file extension .css to indicate what they are. We're going to be working with the HTML template we cleaned up at the beginning of Chapter 10 and adding a bit of formatting to help us experiment with the three layers of CSS – inline, `<style>` element (or internal) and external style sheets. This formatting will be the foundation for formatting a sample web page which you can actually publish on the Internet later if you like.

Each of the three ways to specify a CSS document offers advantages and disadvantages, but the rules and usage are always the same. Once they've been learned, they can be applied anywhere on the document, depending on the desired effect. It's also possible to use inheritance to combine styles and build them up. An external style sheet and an internal style sheet may specify different rules about the same element and, on that page, the rules will be combined. Inline style sheets, however, only allow the specification of rules for a single element, which eliminates some of the powerful selector tools CSS3 offers in external and `<style>` element sheets.

Jargon buster

Inheritance – When one object or element receives its properties or behaviours from a previously existing one, usually as a result of being nested within it.

In Chapter 10, you learned that CSS formatting 'cascades', meaning styles are prioritised from the top down. The lower, or inline styles, have the highest priority, the embedded or internal style sheets are next, while the external style sheets have the lowest priority. There are caveats to this general rule, however, and they will be covered in this chapter. Inheritance of properties is also discussed as we progress through the various strata of CSS layers.

External style sheets are text documents with all the formatting CSS rules set out on them. They are saved with a .css filename extension. Websites link to the external style sheets via the `<link>` element, which is placed in the `<head>` element of the HTML file. The website then retrieves the rules for each of the selectors in the CSS document and applies them to all the pages of a website linked to the CSS file.

The `<link>` element is obviously HTML, not CSS, and is a sort of metadata element. That is, it's included in the `<head>` element of the HTML file and contains non-visual content data. The `<link>` element has several attributes which come into play, but, for our purposes, we will use only two: the `rel` and `href` attributes.

The `rel` attribute defines the relationship between the linked resource and the current page. For instance, for the purposes of this book, the `rel` attribute will always be set to the value `"stylesheet"` as we are linking to style sheets. This need not be the case – you can link to other types of resources, too. The `href` attribute is set to the URL of the style sheet on the web server, and all the rules of relative and absolute URL linking apply. It works in exactly the same way that the `href` attribute does for the `<a>` tag. The `<link>` tag is an empty tag.

The `<link>` element may also have the `type` attribute in it, which will list the type of style sheet the browser should expect in our particular case. The browser can then ignore any unsupported style sheets in favour of those it does support. For the tasks in this book, we use the value `"text/css"`, though other types may be used.

Using an external style sheet has the distinct advantage of being easy to maintain. Changing the look of an entire site can be done from a single location rather than having to alter each individual page or each element of a particular type throughout a website. A single change can have far-reaching impacts. Entire sites can be given a new look and feel with a few simple lines of code added or edited in the .css file.

Creating an external style sheet

Cross reference

See Chapter 4, for more information on the `href` element and relative and absolute URL linking.

For your information

The W3C's and the WHATWG's websites have additional information on the syntax for use with the `<link>` element. Visit **www.w3.org** and **www. whatwg.org** for more details.

Creating an external style sheet (cont.)

External style sheets have their weaknesses as well. You must be careful when using internal or inline styles alongside external style sheets. Because they are the highest level of formatting instruction, all lower levels are either added to their rules or overridden altogether. Depending on the placement in the `<head>` element, internal style sheets might inadvertently supplant an external style sheet. Inheritance can create strange or undesirable effects. If a certain page needs to have a specific appearance, it may be easier to create a lower-level layer of formatting if the page does not change frequently.

For your information

Because style sheets can be quite lengthy, it's advisable to use a text editor to help with the CSS code. Notepad++ offers helpful font- and colour-coordinated identifying tags, which can be customised easily in the program's options. Notepad++ is what has been used in most of the text editor screenshots in this book. Notepad++ has the added benefit of being freeware. That is, there is no charge for its use.

This task provides a visual way to see the effects of an external style sheet which is linked to a sample page and applies formatting to it. In this case, we will apply colour settings to permit the paragraph text to display as blue. Note that the colour formatting will be applied to *all* the `<p>` elements on the sample web page regardless of what structural element contains them. This will also be true for any other web pages linked to the style sheet we will create.

The results here will give immediate feedback on the success or failure of the CSS rule. We will continue to add to the CSS file in future tasks to build our sample web page and improve the look of our basic sample HTML page.

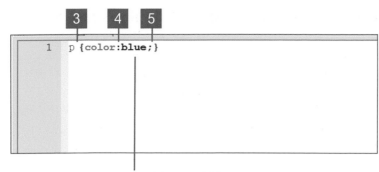

```
1   p {color:blue;}
```

Note the syntax used for the CSS rule. Everything is lower case, the rule is encased in curly brackets and the rule is closed with a semicolon.

Important

Spelling counts in computer code. Unlike a word processing program, such as Microsoft Word, a text editor will not likely have a built-in spell check feature. Even if it does, it may not be able to identify correctly the language settings you use on your local computer and the language requirements for the code you're writing. Be sure you've accurately and correctly spelled any code keywords or selectors, or the code may not work. Spelling is always the first thing to troubleshoot when something isn't working or behaves unexpectedly.

1 Open your sample web page from Chapter 10 in your web browser and view its appearance. Note all the text is black against a white background.

2 Open a new, blank document in your text editor and save it with the filename 'style. css'. This will be your style sheet. Make sure to save it in the same folder on your computer as the sample HTML page you will use for this task.

3 On the first line of the style sheet, type the letter 'p', followed by a space, then an opening curly bracket, like this: 'p {'.

4 In the curly bracket, type 'color:blue'. Note, use the US spelling of 'color' – the rule will not work if it is spelled any other way!

5 Type a semicolon, a closing curly bracket, then save the file and close it.

Creating an external style sheet (cont.)

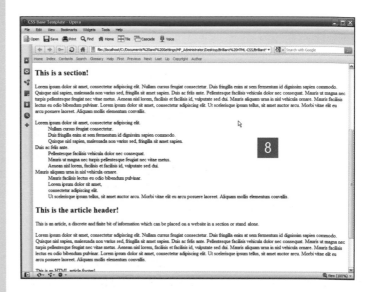

```
1   <!DOCTYPE html SYSTEM "about:legacy-compat">
2   <html>
3
4   <head>
5   <link rel="stylesheet" href="style.css">   7
6   </head>
7
8   <title>CSS Base Template</title>
9
10  <body>
```

6 Open the sample web page HTML template in your text editor and save it with a new name.

7 In the `<head>` element, add the `<link>` element. Add the `rel` attribute and set the value to `"stylesheet"`. Then add the `href` attribute with the value set to `"style.css"`.

8 Return to the sample web page and refresh the view.

The next level of formatting in CSS comes from the internal style sheet. There is almost nothing new to know about an internal style sheet over and above an external one except where it's placed. Instead of using the `<link>` element to link the style sheet to the page, the `<style>` element is added to the `<head>` element in its place. This has the benefit of being on the page to be formatted, but has the disadvantage of formatting only the page where it resides.

The `<style>` element – which is HTML again – tells the browser to expect style information rather than content or metadata. The `<style>` element has the `type` attribute, which is identical to the `type` attribute of the `<link>` element. For our purposes, the value is `"text/css"`. There is, however, no need for `href` or `rel` attributes as the style sheet exists directly on the web page it formats.

After the declaration for the style sheet, the syntax for all the rules remains the same. You don't need to learn a new way to code CSS for an internal style sheet.

The results of this task are also immediately visible. An inline style sheet will be used to format the font colour of a list on our sample web page. The style sheet from the previous task remains to format the `<p>` elements, providing a preview of layered – cascaded – styles. The task results provide immediate diagnostics for the code – if it doesn't work, you won't see the font colour change.

1. Open the sample web page you used in the previous task in your text editor and save it with a new name.

2. In the `<head>` element, add the `<style>` element below the `<link>` element.

3. In the `<style>` element's start tag, add the `type` attribute with the value `"text/css"`.

4. Create a rule for the `<dt>` element: `dt {color:indigo;}`.

5. Create a rule for the `<dd>` element: `dd {color:blueviolet;}`.

6. Add the end tag for the `</style>` element and save the HTML file, then open it in your browser and observe the results.

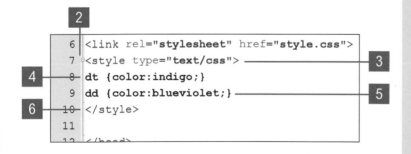

```
 6  <link rel="stylesheet" href="style.css">
 7  <style type="text/css">            ── 3
 8  dt {color:indigo;}
 9  dd {color:blueviolet;}            ── 5
10  </style>
11
12  </head>
```

Creating an internal style sheet (cont.)

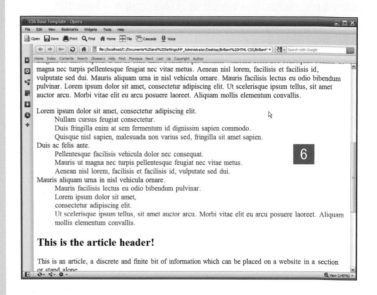

Inline style sheets follow the same rules as the external and internal style sheets in terms of their syntax, but their scope is much more limited. External style sheets can format entire websites and internal style sheets can format an entire page. Inline style sheets, however, can only affect the element to which they are applied.

The limits of the inline style sheet make it the last resort for styling. Obviously, it isn't something a web designer uses, except in special situations, as it requires so much individual work. It does, however, offer styling which overrides all the other style sheets, unless inheritance is accounted for.

Inline style sheets are best for situations where a single element needs to be specially formatted and the content won't change frequently, so, in turn, the code won't need to be redone frequently.

Inline style sheets are declared by the `style` attribute of the element rather than a separate HTML tag. The value for the attribute setting – meaning the entire style sheet – applies the formatting.

Creating an inline style sheet

11

For your information

Inheritance in CSS means rules which are not specified in one style sheet but specified in another are passed to the formatted element anyway. For instance, if you change the font face in the external style sheet and the font colour in an internal style sheet for the same element, both formatting levels are applied. In this way, it is possible to have a particular element inherit formatting from all the three levels of style sheets.

For your information

In previous versions of HTML, a `<span>` or `<div>` element could be used to group certain elements together. With HTML5's much more specific structural elements, however, grouping with these elements isn't as necessary any more, for the most part. Specific styles, however, can still be applied to grouped elements using the `<span>` and `<div>` elements as wrappers for formatting. While they are largely not necessary any more, they are still valid tags and can be used without reservation in modern HTML5 markup.

Creating an inline style sheet (cont.)

In this task, you will add a `style` attribute to a particular element on the sample web page which you modified in the previous task. The style sheet you will create in the attribute allows you to modify a single element on the page and see the results.

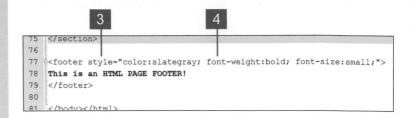

1 Open the sample web page from the previous task in your text editor and save it with a new name.

2 Locate the page footer for the web page (it's the *second* footer on the page).

3 In the start tag for the footer, add the `style` attribute and the double quotes for the value.

4 Inside the double quotes, place the value: `color:slate; font-weight:bold; font-size:small;`. Be sure to end the style value with a semicolon and ensure double quotes close it.

5 Remove the `<h3>` tag from around the content of the footer element.

6 Save the HTML file and open it in a web browser to view the results.

Important

An element nested in another element will cause any formatting of the parent element (the outermost element) to be ignored for the internal element. Special selectors must be used to apply formatting within a nested element.

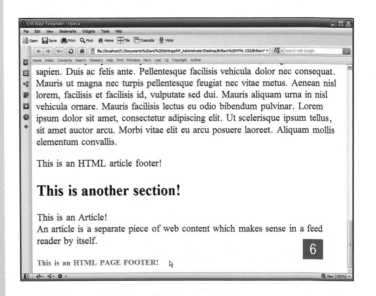

Setting borders with CSS

Introduction

CSS provides formatting options for almost everything on a web page. Borders are part of those formatting options because everything on a web page has a border around its limits, whether it's visible or invisible. CSS provides ways to make the border visible and attractive, one which works fluidly with the scheme of a page.

Think of all the elements on a page as being in a box which acts as a content container. Each container has specific boundaries. Using CSS, it's possible to set those boundaries, expand or contract them, then make them a visible and integral part of page design. Once the idea of HTML structure as a series of boxes is clear in your mind, it becomes a simple matter of seeing other aspects of the elements, such as padding (the space between a box's content and its border) and margins (the space between one box's border and any adjacent box's margin) in the same way.

CSS3 offers exciting new options for using borders with content to create new, visually appealing pages. For example, rounded corners on elements are possible now using a CSS setting rather than other formatting tricks. The use of images as borders is now possible, too. CSS3 provides simple, easy ways to create effects such as drop shadows, which could only be obtained using images created in graphics programs, such as Adobe Photoshop®, previously.

When HTML elements are deeply nested within one another, formatting all the elements can become tricky. CSS3 has new selectors and combinators, however, which allow the

What you'll do

Add a border to an element

Create borders using separate lines

Create rounded corners on a border

Use an image as a border

application of formatting to specific parts of HTML structures and, when necessary, the `<div>` and `<span>` elements can be called on to great effect. In all, CSS3 allows very flexible and dynamic formatting application, so very interesting and attractive web designs are possible, more easily than ever before.

Jargon buster

Combinator – CSS code operators which are placed between simple selectors to allow granular selection of elements for formatting on a web page.

Simple selector – The portion of a CSS rule which selects the element to be formatted. Simple selectors select only one element at a time without targeting their parent or child elements.

One of the basic things to learn about when working with CSS borders is, of course, the borders themselves. A border is the outline of an element's shape on the page. They're rectangular and composed of lines and, with CSS, it's the lines which are formatted. They can be dotted, dashed or solid lines, combinations of dots and dashes and even images can be used instead of lines.

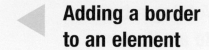

Table 12.1 CSS property used in this task

Property	Function
border	Sets the border for a selected element. Uses the settings for size, line style and colour.

Adding borders is simple and offers the eye ready and easily recognisable divisions between portions of HTML pages, such as sections and articles or headings and footers. Different blog posts on a single page, for example, might be separated by each having their own individual border. The page itself can also be divided into content and sidebars with border schemes.

It's also possible to control individual parts of a border. For instance, it's possible to set the bottom border to be different from the others or for only the top or sides of the border to be visible. Borders can be heavy on one side and thin on the other three. The combinations are myriad, but control of the borders of elements can make the difference between a page which is exciting for the eye and one which is confusing and boring.

The results of this task show immediately and provide positive visual proof of your work. Borders appear around the <h1> elements on the page.

Adding a border to an element (cont.)

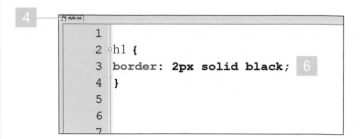

1. Open the sample web page you made in the previous chapter in your text editor. Be sure to use one without inline or internal style sheets on it.

2. Save the web page with a new name and, if possible, to a new location and close it.

3. Open the newly saved web page on your web browser.

4. Open the style.css text file you created in the last chapter in your text editor. If possible, save it with a new name (but retain the .css file extension) to the same location as the sample web page.

5. Remove all formatting instructions from style.css and save.

6. Create the following rule for all `<h1>` elements:

```
h1 {
border: 2px solid
black;
}
```

7. Save the style.css file, then refresh the sample web page in your browser to view the results.

For your information

Moving the file locations allows the `<link>` element created previously to link to the style.css file from the sample web page without overlapping the style sheet formatting of another sheet named style.css.

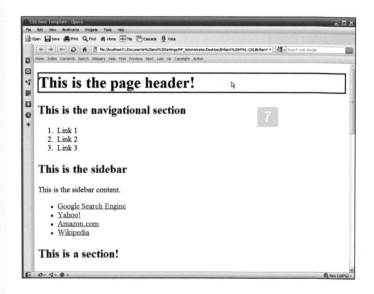

The rule you created for the `<h1>` element in the previous task used a single declaration which named several properties:

```
h1 {
border: 2px solid black;
}
```

This rule formats three different aspects of the border at once: the border width (2px), type (solid) and colour (black). This is a convenient way to declare a CSS rule, but it only works if all the lines in the border are the same width, style and colour. What if you want to vary the border lines somehow?

Table 12.2 CSS properties used in this task

Property	Function
`border-top-width` `border-right-width` `border-left-width` `border-bottom-width`	Sets the border width in either pixels or as the values **thick**, **thin** or **medium** for a selected element.

To format the appearance of a border with greater control, CSS provides properties for each of the lines in the border. It's possible to set the lines' colour, style and width separately. Rather than a *generic* border property, each of the properties can then be set with its *own* CSS property:

```
h1 {
border-left-color: black;
border-right-color: blue;
border-bottom-style: dotted;
border-top-width: 5px;
}
```

By setting each of the border properties separately, different look and feel combinations can be achieved on a single web page. Different elements can be made to stand out from others just by enhancing their borders in various ways.

Creating borders using separate lines

12

Creating borders using separate lines (cont.)

1. Open the style.css file in your text editor.

2. Create a rule for the `<header>` element to place a border around the page header. Make the top, right and left borders 1px each and the bottom border 5px.

```
header {
border-top-width:
1px;
border-right-width:
1px;
border-left-width:
1px;
border-bottom-
width: 5px;
}
```

3. In the same way, create a rule for `<article>` elements which creates a dashed border of 2px around all sides. Make the borders grey – 'gray' in the code as needs to be US spelling!

```
article {
border: 2px dashed
gray;
}
```

This task represents a challenge, because the nesting of elements can create problems if not handled properly. In this case, the nested elements in the target elements will not be accounted for as they were in the previous task. Then, the formatting didn't work as well. Using proper combinators and selectors – or even 'wrapper' elements such as `<div>` and `<span>` – however, as we will here, we can overcome those challenges. The point of this task is for you to practise coding CSS rules and show you how different formatting elements impact a style sheet.

```
  1
  2  h1 {
  3  border: 2px solid black;
  4  }
  5
  6  header {
  7  border-top-width: 1px;
  8  border-right-width: 1px;
  9  border-left-width: 1px;
 10  border-bottom-width: 5px;
 11  }
 12
 13  div {
 14  border: 2px dashed gray;
 15  }
 16
 17
 18
```

Creating borders using separate lines (cont.)

4 Save the style.css file, but don't close it. Open the sample web page you created for the previous task in your web browser and observe the results.

5 Add a `<div>` element around the first `<article>` element in the HTML file for the sample web page and save the HTML file with a new name. Be sure the `<div>` start tag comes before the `<article>` start tag and the `</div>` end tag comes after the `</article>` end tag.

6 Add a rule to the style.css file to put the same dashed border around the `<div>` element.

For your information

You could also create a rule for the `<article>` elements, using individual border properties as you have for the `<header>` element. Both will work.

Important

Note that, in step 4, the header borders don't change and only the footer of the article has the expected dashed line around it. That is because elements nested in the selected elements don't receive the CSS rules we have applied. In step 5, we correct the problem with the `<article>` border by using a `<div>` tag to encompass all the other elements inside the `<article>` element. We will fix the `<header>` tag in Chapter 14.

Creating borders using separate lines (cont.)

7 Save the style.css file and open the newly saved sample web page in the browser to see the results.

Timesaver tip

Simply change the name of the rule from 'article' to 'div' and save the style.css file again to change the rule from applying to the `<article>` element to applying to any `<div>` element.

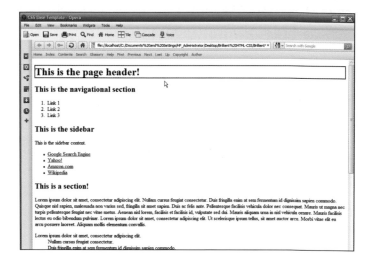

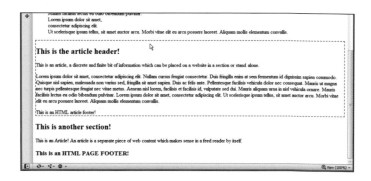

One of the nice things about CSS3 is the ability to create rounded corners for borders without having to create an image in software such as Adobe Photoshop® first and use it instead of borders. While you *can* use images as borders (see the next task), it's nice to be able to bend the lines around the corners of a border without needing to be an artist or hire one.

The property for doing this is **border-radius**, when all four corners will have the same radius. The radius value is expressed as pixels. The corners can be rounded individually as well, using the following properties:

```
border-top-right-radius
border-bottom-right-radius
border-top-left-radius
border-bottom-left-radius
```

The units for the individual measurements are in pixels once more.

Table 12.3 CSS property used in this task

Property	Function
border-radius	Sets the radius of the rounded-off corner for the selected element's border in pixels. This property requires all four corners be set consecutively, with no comma separators (**border-radius: 20px 20px 15px 15px;**, for example).

Using the **border-radius** property is simple and easily visible, as the results of the following task will show. It can add a nice dimension to your web page designs.

For your information

Some care should be exercised when using the **border-radius** properties. Remember, not all browsers have adopted the standard yet and not all computer monitors have the same resolution. Make the radius too small and it may not be noticeable; make it too large and you can compromise the content. Experiment with different computer resolutions and degrees of radius when designing your web pages until you find the appearance pleasing.

Creating rounded corners on a border (cont.)

1. Open your style.css file in your text editor, then open your sample web page from the last task in your text editor and save it with a new name.

2. Open the HTML file you just saved in your text editor and close the old file to avoid confusion. Open it on your web browser also.

3. Add a rule to the style sheet to select the page footer element only. Do this with the combinator `body > footer`.

4. Create a rule for the `<footer>` element which applies a corner radius of 12px to all four corners. Set the border to 2px, solid line style and 'gray' for the colour.

5. Save the style.css file and refresh the sample web page in the browser.

```
1
2  h1 {
3      border: 2px solid black;
4  }
5
6  body > footer {          3
7      border: 2px solid gray;
8      border-top-right-radius: 12px;
9      border-bottom-right-radius: 12px;    4
10     border-top-left-radius: 12px;
11     border-bottom-left-radius: 12px;
12 }
13
14
```

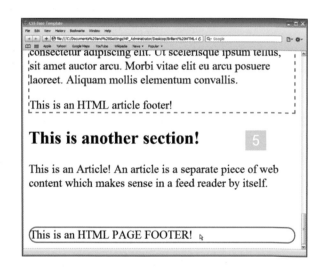

So far, you've learned how to apply borders to elements in two different ways. You've also learned you can create variable borders using CSS properties. There are a great many things you can do with borders using CSS – we have only seen a fraction here. There are loads of other properties you can experiment with as you create style sheets for web pages.

Table 12.4 CSS properties used in this task

Property	Function
border-image	Points to the image to be used and sets how it is to be spread over the selected element's border. Requires the **url** setting and four image 'slice' sizes to apply the image to the border. Also requires the **repeat** type used for the image between corners to be set, to **none**, **stretch**, **round** or **repeat**. Use this in conjunction with the **border-width** property.
border-width	Sets the width of a border for the selected element in pixels or as **thin**, **medium** or **thick** fixed values.

CSS3 permits borders which aren't lines of any sort. You can apply images to elements as a border, for example. An image is set as a border using the **border-image** property settings, which are divided into three parts and used in conjunction with the **border-width** property.

The **border-image** property rule looks like this:

```
border-image: url('diagram.png') N N N
N horizontalrepeat verticalrepeat;
```

The first part of the property is the declaration, of course. The second part specifies the image to be used as the border. It's not quite as simple as it first appears, however, as the image chosen will be 'sliced' into nine parts for the border, according to the settings in the rule. Confused? Don't be,

Using an image as a border

12

Cross reference

Refer to the quick reference guide for CSS properties (downloaded from **www.veign.com**) or other online resources for more details of CSS border properties.

Important

Not all CSS3 recommendations have been adopted as standard for all browsers at this time, so you may not be able to see the results of this task in your browser.

Using an image as a border (cont.)

as it will become clear shortly. For now, just know the first part of this rule points to the image to be used.

The second part of the rule (designated as 'N' in the example above) consists of sizes (the 'N's are replaced with digits) which define how the image is sliced up. This determines the height and width of the border.

The third part of the rule defines how the slices are placed on the border. The settings are `stretch`, `repeat`, `round` and `none`. The `stretch` setting will take a single slice of the image and stretch it along the border. The `repeat` setting will repeat the image slice as many times as possible to complete the border. The `round` setting will also repeat the slice, but does so in such a way that there are no cut off, or partial, slices along the border. `None`, of course, is self-explanatory. Note there are two values: the first is the horizontal repeat type and the second the vertical repeat type.

I hope the concept seems clearer now! To offer more clarity, note the way in which the image is sliced looks like a noughts and crosses board:

A		B
D		C

'A' represents one corner, 'B' another, 'C' the third and 'D' the final one. 'A' to 'D' can be designated as pixel numbers or percentages relative to the size of the image used. 'A' and 'C' represent height while 'B' and 'D' represent width. The top border can be a different width from the bottom one using these control settings.

With those facts in mind, the `border-image` property is a shorthand version of the properties:

```
border-top-image
border-bottom-image
border-right-image
border-left-image
```

An accompanying property is `border-corner-image`, which is a shortened version of the following:

```
border-top-left-image
border-top-right-image
border-bottom-left-image
border-bottom-right-image
```

The individual settings can be used to achieve finer control over how the border image appears on the page. Images such as the one below are probably the most useful and easiest to control.

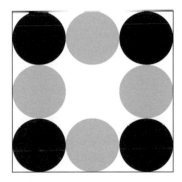

This can be sliced into segments easily and logically and the sizing of the slices is simple. All you need to know is how big each of the 'slices' you'd like to use is and the centre of the image becomes the space for the content. In the image above, each of the circles is 200px wide in the original .png file. Using that number in my `border-image` property in this task, the border image can be placed around the `<header>` element.

Using an image as a border (cont.)

```
14
15  body > header {
16  border-width: 5px;
17  border-image: url('border.png') 200 200 200 200 stretch round;
18  }
19
```

1 Open your style.css file in your text editor. Open your sample web page in your text editor and save it with a new name.

2 In the style.css file, change the rule for the **<header>** element to use an image for the border. Use the combinator in the selector to choose only the **<header>** for the page, not one nested in another element. To do this, add the selector for the parent element of the element you wish to select (in this case, the **<body>** element), and use a 'greater-than' symbol followed by the selector for the element you're formatting (in this case, the **<header>**), as shown:

```
body > header {
border-width: 5px;
border-image: url
('border.png') 200
200 200 200 stretch
round;
}
```

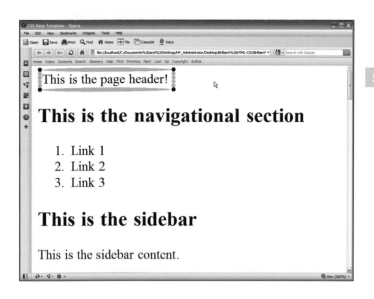

3 To make the `<heading>` element formatting work, remove the `<h1>` element within the `<header>` element on the newly saved sample web page's HTML file, then refresh the view.

4 Save the style.css file.

5 Open your HTML file in the browser and view the results. Remember, not all browsers can properly display the `border-image` property formatting.

6 If you like, change the `<header>` element CSS rule back to its previous state if your browser(s) does not properly display the border image.

12

Formatting colours and backgrounds with CSS

Introduction

Web design and web programming are very different fields. Web design is less technical and has to do with aesthetics and what is pleasing and functional. A website has to look good to retain viewers and draw traffic. It must also be functional and intuitive. Designing a web page which looks and feels good to those using it is what web design is all about.

A big part of web design is choosing the right colour scheme for the website. Colours, complementary colours, contrasting colours, accenting colours – all sorts of choices must be made. Sometimes these can be done instinctively. Other times it may help to study colour theory a bit to understand how different colours might impact viewers.

At one time on the Internet, technology limited the display of colours. Those days, however, are long over. Monitors are now capable of displaying thousands or millions of colours, even if the human eye cannot detect the subtle differences. Web designers aren't limited by the technology any more in terms of the colour palette they can create. So the world of web design has opened up dramatically as advances in displays and graphics capabilities have been made.

CSS offers several ways to format colours for a web page. Elements can have colours applied universally or to each one, as required. Tremendous control can be applied to colours by different colour specification methods, including colour names and hexadecimal numbering. There is almost no limit to the items CSS can apply colours to on a web page.

What you'll do

Choose a colour palette

Specify CSS colours four ways

Set foreground and background colours

Set background images

Choosing a colour palette unaided can be daunting, though. Colours for a website are critical. They affect how a site is perceived, convey an image or brand, can be an extension of a company's presence and promote or detract from the desired 'feel' of a site. Together with fonts and graphics, colours are a powerful element in the creation of a site. The choices made are important, especially for professional websites. Not everyone is equally able when it comes to choosing a colour palette, especially when it can mean the difference between a site which is well-received, conveying professionalism and a clean look, and a poorly received, quickly abandoned site with few repeat visitors.

Fortunately, tools exist which can help those less familiar with colour theory to create a pleasing colour palette for website use. Some of those tools are online and others come as downloadable desktop tools. They belong in the arsenal of any web designer.

CSS colours are specified using RGB, hexadecimal or name values. To provide some idea of how advances in technology have opened up colour schemes for designers, as of 2009, no fewer than 74 per cent of web users had 32-bit colour capabilities. The 16-bit capability provides 65,536 colour choices, while 32 bits provides 16,777,216 colour choices.

There are two important design considerations when choosing your site's colours. First, the ability to use thousands of colours doesn't mean you can ignore aesthetics. Some colours look good together and others don't. Second, many monitors, for various reasons, do not display colours accurately in all cases, and may not display subtle colour differences correctly. You might spend hours choosing a subtle, artistic colour combination which doesn't display well for all users. Aim for contrast rather than subtle colour differences. Contrast does not mean your site must be garish, however. Be sure to stay within the palette you've selected.

This task is straightforward. You will enter a base colour and produce a complementary palette relating to that colour. Alternatively, you can use an online tool to find sets of complementary colour schemes in warm, cool and neutral ranges.

If you feel capable of selecting a strong, pleasing colour palette without the use of a tool, you don't have to use one. Knowing where to locate these types of tools, however, is beneficial to any web designer.

Choosing a colour palette

13

!

Important

When using a desktop palette selection tool, remember, subtle colour differences may not render well on some users' monitors. It is best, therefore, to go for more rather than less colour contrast.

Choosing a colour palette (cont.)

1 Open your web browser.

2 Navigate to the Color Schemer Online colour palette tool at: **http://colorschemer.com/online.html**.

3 Enter #B22222 (firebrick) as the hexadecimal value and click **Set HEX**.

4 Note the set of complementary colours produced. Selecting from these colours will ensure your website will look appealing.

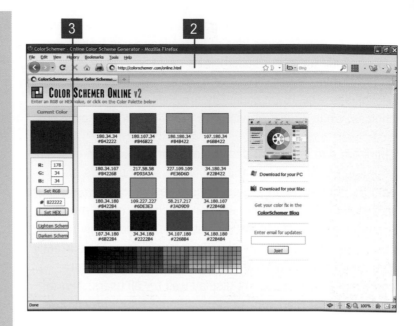

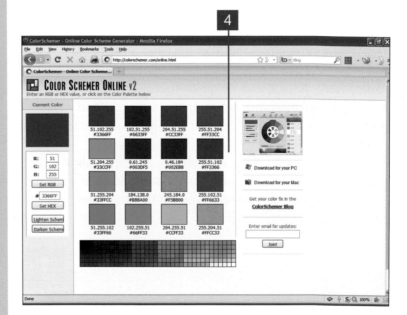

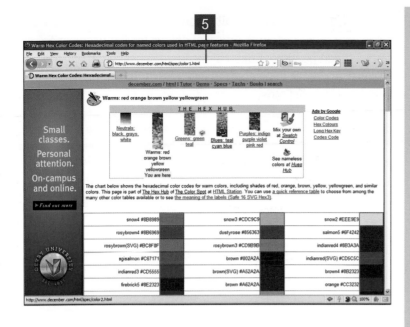

Choosing a colour palette (cont.)

5 Now navigate to December. com at: **www.december.com**.

6 On the homepage, click **Hex Hub** in the 'Encounter' box.

7 In **The Hex Hub** box, you can select a predefined palette in the warms or neutrals ranges, for example.

8 Click on the 'a quick reference table' link to see an abbreviated list of colours from the full list and see all 4800+ colours available from this site.

9 Notice the site provides the hexadecimal numbers and the name values for the colours shown in the table.

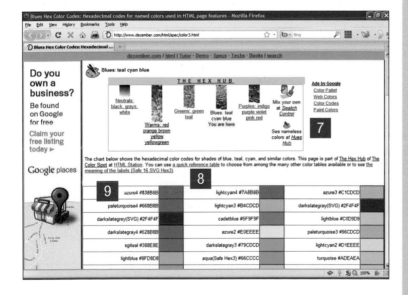

13

Specifying CSS colours four ways

In order to change the default colour for any element on a web page, you must specify a different colour for the browser to apply. It can be almost any colour (as discussed earlier, the number of colour choices available soars into the millions), but you must pick one.

Table 13.1 The names, RGB and hexadecimal values of a few colours

Name	Code name	RGB value	Hexadecimal value
Asparagus	asparagus	rgb(123,160,91)	#7BA05B
Alice Blue	aliceblue	rgb(240,248,255)	#f0f8ff
Blanched Almond	blanchedalmond	rgb(255,235,205)	#ffebcd
Turquoise	turquoise	rgb(64,224,208)	#40e0d0

There are four ways to specify CSS colours. The first is to use the colour's name.

```
color: cornflowerblue;
```

The second way is to specify a colour by its hexadecimal value.

```
color: #6495ED
```

The third and fourth ways involve using RGB values for a colour. RGB stands for 'red green blue' and the values signify the amounts of red, green and blue in the colours. There are two ways to express RGB values. The first is by the percentages of red, green and blue in the colour.

```
color: rgb(39%,58%,93%);
```

The second is by specifying RGB colour values directly.

```
color: rgb(100,149,237);
```

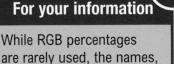

Important

Hexadecimal values are case-sensitive. Be careful to enter them correctly when specifying a colour by hex.

For your information

While RGB percentages are rarely used, the names, hexadecimal values and RGB values are all commonly used.

In this task, you will assign a colour value to certain heading borders on your sample web page. The results are straightforward. The borders should look as specified in the CSS sheet.

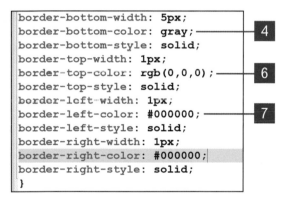

```
border-bottom-width: 5px;
border-bottom-color: gray;           4
border-bottom-style: solid;
border-top-width: 1px;
border-top-color: rgb(0,0,0);        6
border-top-style: solid;
border-left-width: 1px;
border-left-color: #000000;          7
border-left-style: solid;
border-right-width: 1px;
border-right-color: #000000;
border-right-style: solid;
}
```

1 Open the style.css and HTML files for the sample web page created in the last chapter in your text editor. Save the HTML file with a new name.

2 Open your newly saved HTML file in your web browser.

3 In the style.css file, locate the `body > header` CSS rule and remove the `border-image` property. Be sure to leave the `border-width` property intact.

13

4 Add a property to the `body > header` rule to declare the bottom border of the header as `gray`, specifying the colour by the colour value of `gray`. Then add the `border-bottom-style` of `solid` to the rule.

```
body > header {
border-bottom-width:
5px;
border-bottom-color:
gray;
border-bottom-style:
solid;
}
```

Specifying CSS colours four ways (cont.)

Timesaver tip

The copy and paste function is your friend! Where multiple, identical rules are to be created and a single declaration cannot be made for them, don't hesitate to copy and paste your properties from one rule to another to save you typing them all repeatedly.

5 Save the style.css file and refresh the web page in your browser to view the results.

6 Add the same three CSS properties (width, colour and style) for the top border. Make the width 1px and the colour value rgb(0,0,0).

7 Add the width, colour and style properties for the left and right borders also, making the width 1px for both and the colour value #000000. Do not leave off the leading hash (#) mark.

8 Save the style.css file and refresh your web page in your browser to view the results.

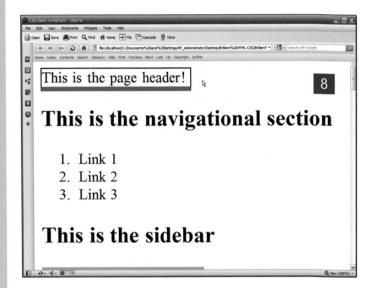

Declaring a foreground colour for an element using CSS is simple. The element's colour is declared in a rule. There's nothing else to it – just declare the colour!

```
body {color: lime;}
```

In general, the foreground of an element is the text content. The `color` property therefore applies to text for the most part. This includes formatting HTML tags such as `<em>`, `<strong>`, and `<sup>`.

```
strong {color: red;}
em {color: #E3372E;}
```

Any element can have a colour declared. Setting the colour for an element without *text* content (like a horizontal rule), however, has no effect. Remember this rule of thumb: no text, no colour; text, colour.

Table 13.2 CSS properties covered in this task

Property	Function
color	Specifies an element's foreground, or text, colour.
background-color	Specifies an element's background colour.

In this task, the page's body background will be coloured while certain heading tags will have backgrounds coloured dark grey and foregrounds coloured white.

For your information

The colour for a single element or particular text can be overridden by setting the text colour for a paragraph element or using an inline style sheet.

Setting foreground and background colours (cont.)

Any element can have a background colour. CSS makes background colours possible by means of its `background-color` declaration. The declared colour is displayed as the background colour of the element selected in CSS.

Elements which format content in some way – such as heading elements (`h1-h6`) or even `<p>` elements – may not receive or inherit the background of the parent element. If the parent element has content (such as text) which does not have a formatting element wrapper, then the element's background colour shows through.

For instance, if you put text into an `<article>` element and set the `background-color` for it to a certain colour, that colour will be visible behind any content in the `<article>` element (depending on browser support). If, however, you put `<p>` elements around the text content within the `<article>` element, only content which is not in a `<p>` element will have the `<article>` background colour.

For your information

The Opera™ web browser does not show a background colour in nested formatting elements. The Safari browser (for Windows), however, does show the background chosen for the parent element for any nested elements. That is, the backgrounds of nested elements are transparent if a background colour isn't declared and the background for the parent element is visible.

Important

The concept of background colour for nested elements is important. A web page may not look as intended if the formatting is not applied to some content because of nested elements.

It's normal practice to vary background colours on different parts of a web page to assist with clarity, legibility or draw attention to things. Most web pages do not have much more than simple black-on-white or black-on-grey schemes for text content, but, occasionally, a white-on-black or white-on-grey page will be used, particularly for individuals' websites and blogs. The bright text against a dark background is a bit harder on the eyes for most viewers, so this scheme is used less frequently on commercial websites.

1 Open the style.css file in your text editor, then open your sample web page in the text editor and save it with a new name.

2 Open the sample web page you just saved in your web browser.

3 In the style sheet, at the top of the sheet (above the other rules), add a CSS declaration which sets the **<body>** element's background colour to the value 'darkgray'.

4 Add a rule to the style sheet which changes text for all the heading elements – **<h1>** to **<h6>** – to the value 'gray' for the background and the foreground colour set to the value 'white'.

13

For your information

If a CSS rule changing the **<aside>** element's background to the value 'palegreen' still exists on your style sheet, remove it now. Do the same with the dashed border for the **<div>** element.

Setting foreground and background colours (cont.)

5 Save the style sheet file and refresh the page in your web browser to view the results.

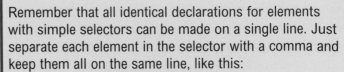

Timesaver tip

Remember that all identical declarations for elements with simple selectors can be made on a single line. Just separate each element in the selector with a comma and keep them all on the same line, like this:

`h1, h2, h3 {cssproperty rule;}`

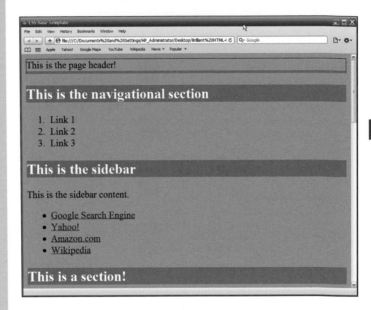

5

Any element can have an image as its background. Simply use the CSS **background-image** property.

```
body {background-image: url(./myimage.
png);}
```

Table 13.3 CSS background-image properties

Property	Function
background-image: url(path)	Specifies a background image for an element.
background-repeat: repeat	Specifies a background image is tiled.
background-repeat: repeat-y	Specifies a background image is tiled vertically.
background-repeat: repeat-x	Specifies a background image is tiled horizontally.
background-repeat: no-repeat	Specifies a background image does not repeat.
background-attachment: fixed	Specifies a background image not scroll with a page, but is a fixed background.
background-attachment: scroll	Specifies a background image scrolls with the page.
background-position:	Specifies a background image's position on the page.

A background image can be tiled horizontally across the page:

```
<style>
body {
background-image: url(./cyclist27b.tif);
background-repeat: repeat-x;
}
</style>
```

Setting background images

13

Setting background images (cont.)

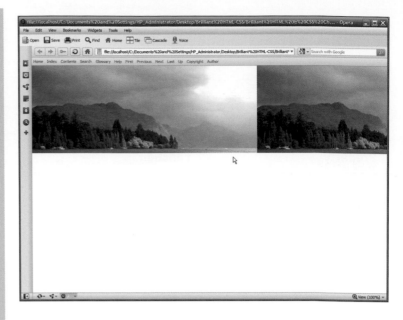

Alternatively it can be tiled vertically:

```
<style type="text/css">
body {
background-image: url(./cyclist27b.tif);
background-repeat: repeat-y;
}
</style>
```

The image can also be centred on the page:

```
<style type="text/css">
body {
background-image: url(./cyclist27.tif);
background-repeat:no-repeat;
background-position: top center;
}
</style>
```

The outcome from this task is clear. The image chosen will be repeated across the screen according to the properties set in the CSS rule. The image used for the task will not look good with our formatted sample web page, but the results shown give you an idea of what can be done with images and backgrounds.

Important

Do not use the HTML file created here for any subsequent tasks. If you like, you can remove the internal style sheet from the HTML file and continue to use it or else use the HTML file from the previous task for subsequent tasks. The background image used in this task may present visual clarity issues if you try to use it in subsequent tasks.

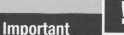

Cross reference

Consult the quick reference guide you downloaded earlier from **www.veign.com** for more background code snippets which can be used to set backgrounds.

13

Setting background images (cont.)

1. Open the sample web page you created in the last task in your text editor and save it with a new name.

2. Add a `<style>` element to the `<head>` element of the newly saved HTML file.

3. Add the style sheet to set the background image: `body {background-image: url(pathtoimage);}`

4. Save the HTML file and open it in your web browser to view the results.

5. Change the internal style sheet code so the image is tiled horizontally on the page by adding the `background-repeat: repeat-x` property to the rule, as shown earlier in this chapter.

6. Save the HTML file and refresh the view in your web browser to see the result of the change.

For your information

You will not be editing the style.css file for this task. As formatting from both the external and internal style sheets will be applied by the browser, you can either remove the `<link>` element from the HTML file being used here or place the `<style>` element after the `<link>` element to ensure the formatting is applied properly.

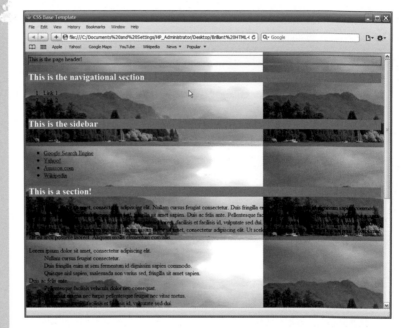

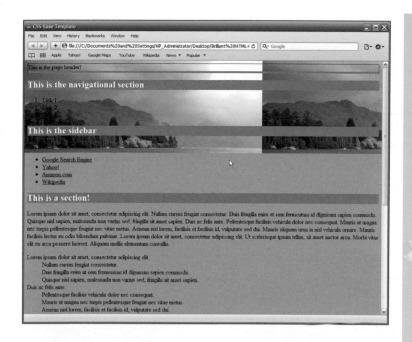

7 Change the HTML's internal style sheet again by changing the `background-repeat` property to `repeat-y`, to tile the image vertically on the page.

8 Save the HTML file again and view the result in your browser.

13

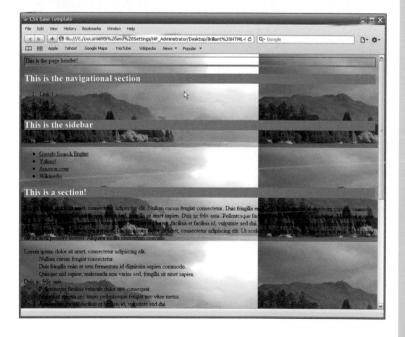

Setting background images (cont.)

```
6  <style>
7
8  body {
9  background-image: url(background.png);
10 background-repeat: no-repeat;
11 background-position: top center;
12 }
13
14 </style>
```

9 Change the `background-repeat` property to `no-repeat` and add the `background-position` property to the rule so the image is centred on the page.

10 Save the HTML file and refresh the view on the browser to see the effect of the changes.

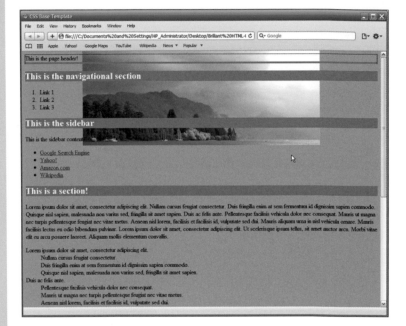

Formatting fonts and text with CSS

Introduction

Fonts are fundamental to all written communication. Fonts convey emotion, style and help your writing convey implicit meaning. For instance, a common web convention is that using all caps indicates SHOUTING.

Consider the different moods the following text samples evoke:

Welcome to my site (Comic Sans)
Welcome to my site (Arial)
Welcome to my site (Garamond)

The Comic Sans font conveys the impression of a loose and informal site, while Arial seems more formal. The Garamond font seems the most formal of the three.

All three font choices would give users different expectations of a site's content. Commercial sites may use Arial, but a news site might choose a Times or Century font. If a rock band's site used Arial, it would seem tame, perhaps even boring. Would you conduct serious online business on a site which used Comic Sans? The impressions given are largely dependent on the look and feel of the site as much as (if not more than!) its functionality. Fonts must be chosen carefully.

Fonts used on a site should be found on most operating systems. If a user's operating system doesn't have a font installed which the page specifies, the browser displays the user's default font set. Those hours agonising over font choices then becomes wasted time. Users will likely view the site in Times, Courier or some other equally mundane font.

What you'll do

Set an element's font family

Set an element's font style

Set a font's weight and size

Set font properties using the font declaration

Decorate text and change case

Align text

Format text using word and letter spacing

Add drop shadows to text

Table 14.1 CSS `font` properties covered in this chapter

Property	Function
font-family	Specifies the font family to be used. The font family can be either a specific family name or a generic font family.
font-style	Specifies the font's style to be normal, italic or oblique.
font-weight	Specifies a font's weight.
font-size	Specifies a font's size.
font	Sets the family, style, weight and size all in one declaration.

CSS provides properties which replace deprecated HTML text formatting tags and attributes, such as the paragraph element's `align` attribute and the underline (`<u></u>`) tags. There are other formatting choices available too, many of which were impossible using HTML attributes.

In this chapter, CSS properties will be used to underline, overline and cross out (strikethrough) text, as well as change its case and cause it to flash. Text alignment and spacing will also be covered. These properties, combined with CSS font properties, are how HTML text is properly formatted.

A font family is declared by the `font-family` property. A font family is a set of fonts which have a similar look to them. For instance, Arial, Courier, and Times New Roman are all font family examples. A generic font family name may also be used to declare the font family. Generic font family names include serif, sans serif, cursive, fantasy and monospace. Generic font families are common to all browsers on all computers and are the safest choice if you want to be certain all users will have the font you specify.

When declaring a font family, more than one font can be listed to ensure users' systems will have the font family needed. Browsers look at each font family in the list and will display one which matches what their systems have.

When using `font-family`, it's good practice to end the list with one of the five generic font family values. Browsers are then provided with multiple options. If Arial isn't on a browser's system, say, it will use Tahoma. If Tahoma can't be found, then it will use sans serif. Because sans serif is a generic font family, it is guaranteed to be there.

```
p {font-family: arial, tahoma,
sans-serif;}
```

Elements inherit font families from parent elements, but have the ability to override the parent's font. The best way to specify fonts is to assign the `<body>` a `font-family` so the pages all share the same base font. Paragraphs, headings and other specific element fonts can override the body element's font.

Setting an element's font family

14

Setting an element's font family (cont.)

Table 14.2 Generic font families and examples of members of those font families

Generic font family	Font families belonging to generic families
Cursive	Comic Sans MS, Apple Chancery, URW Chancery, Monotype Corsiva, Bradley Hand ITC
Fantasy	Impact, Papyrus, Marker Felt, Felix Titling
Monospace	Courier, Courier New, Lucida Console, Monaco, Free Mono
Sans-Serif	Microsoft Sans Serif, Arial, Helvetica, Veranda, Liberation Sans
Serif	Palatino Linotype, Georgia, Times New Roman, Baskerville, American Typewriter

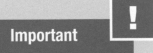

Important

The `font-family` property is only one aspect of an element's font. Its weight, size and style also must be set. We will do this in subsequent tasks, but this task focuses solely on font families.

The results of this task are straightforward. The `font-family` declarations will set the font for the entire sample web page as Arial. If Arial does not exist on a system viewing the page, the browser will use the sans-serif font family set in its preferences.

```
 1
 2   body {
 3     background-color: whitesmoke;
 4     font-family: arial, sans-serif;      2
 5   }
 6
 7   h1, h2, h3 {
 8     background-color: gray;
 9     color: white;
10   }
11
12   body > footer {
13     border: 2px solid gray;
14     border-top-right-radius: 12px;
15     border-bottom-right-radius: 12px;
16     border-top-left-radius: 12px;
17     border-bottom-left-radius: 12px;
18     color: white;
19     background-color: darkgray;          4
20   }
21
22   body > header {
23     border-bottom-width: 5px;
24     border-bottom-color: gray;
25     border-bottom-style: solid;
26     border-top-width: 1px;
27     border-top-color: rgb(0,0,0);
28     border-top-style: solid;
29     border-left-width: 1px;
30     border-left-color: rgb(0,0,0);
31     border-left-style: solid;
32     border-right-width: 1px;
33     border-right-color: #000000;
34     border-right-style: solid;
35     color: white;
36     background-color: darkgray;          3
37   }
38
39   dl {
40     font-family: Times New Roman, serif;  5
41   }
```

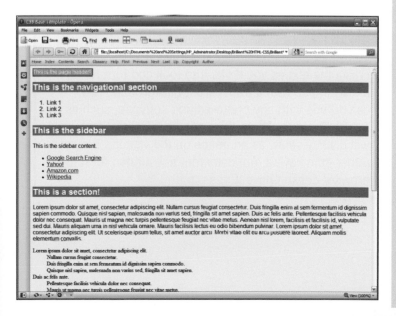

1 Open the style.css file and the sample web page you created in the previous chapter in your text editor. Save the HTML file with a new name.

2 In the style.css file, add a `font-family` declaration to the `body` rule so that the body's default font is Arial: `font-family: arial, sans-serif;`.

3 Add declarations to the page's header rule so that the text is white and the background is darkgray: `color: white; background-colour: darkgray;`.

4 Add the same declarations to, the page's footer rule.

5 Create a rule which assigns Times New Roman text to the `<dl>` element: `dl {font-family: Times New Roman, serif;}`.

6 Save the style sheet and open the HTML file in your web browser to view the results.

14

Setting an element's font family (cont.)

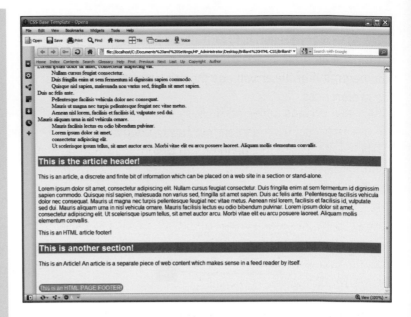

Important

When using `font-family`, if the font's name has white space in it, enclose the `font-family` value in single or double quotations.

```
p{font-family:
"DejaVu Sans";}
```

For your information

Not *all* fonts exist on *all* computer systems. If you install a particularly clever font and then use it in a web page design, it will look fine when loaded on your browser, but what will visitors to your site see? Most probably, they will see *their* browser's *default* font, not the clever font designated, because not all visitors (if any) will have that font installed on their systems.

To use an uncommon font and make it Web-safe, create the text as you'd like it to look and turn it into a PNG image with a transparent background. You can do this with any photo-editing software, such as Adobe Photoshop®. In this way, your interesting text will display safely as an image on the visitor's browser rather than have a mundane font substituted for it if the browser doesn't have access to it.

Font styles are how the font is rendered. There are three standard styles: normal, italic or oblique. Many fonts also have bold and bold italic styles. All fonts have a normal style, which is the default if the `font-style` declaration is omitted.

Italic and oblique styles both cause the text to be altered in a similar 'slanted' fashion, but have subtle differences. Italicised fonts are independent fonts from their normal style counterparts and may have special character designs for certain characters which differ from the normal style. Arial Italic, for example, is an independent system font. When a browser is instructed to load Arial Italic it loads the Arial Italic system font rather than 'italicising' the Arial font. In contrast, the oblique value for Arial may simply display the normal font at a slant, though not necessarily.

Table 14.3 CSS `font-style` properties

Property	Function
`font-style: normal`	Specifies a font's normal style.
`font-style:italic`	Specifies a font's italic style.
`font-style:oblique`	Instructs the browser to slant a font's normal style.

Not all fonts have the same styles available and not all systems have all styles for all the fonts they do have installed. That means a browser may not be able to format in the expected way for every visitor. That, however, is a risk inherent in all web design.

This task's results may hold a surprise. The italics property setting will work as expected, but not the oblique setting. The oblique setting will transform the text in the `<dt>` elements into the italic font rather than simply slanting the original font. This happens when an italic font exists on the system, but may not be universally true.

Setting an element's font style

Cross reference

Remember, many HTML tags change the appearance of text. In many situations these tags are more appropriate than specifying a font. See Chapter 3 for more information on HTML text formatting tags.

14

Setting an element's font style (cont.)

```
38
39  dl {font-family: Times New Roman, serif;}
40
41  dt {font-style: oblique;}
42                                      2
43  dd {font-style: italic;}
44
```

1. Open the HTML page from the previous task in your web browser and open the style.css file in your text editor.

2. Create a rule for the `<dt>` element of an oblique font style and for the `<dd>` element of an italic font style.

3. Save the style.css file and open the HTML file in your web browser to view the results.

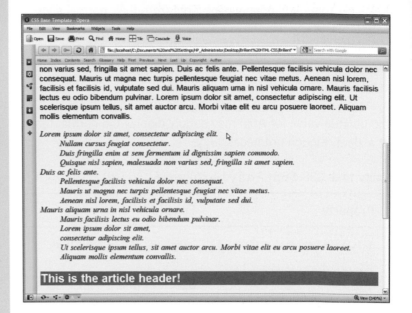

The terms 'weight' and 'size' refer to different aspects of how a font is rendered. A font's weight is how thickly, or how heavily, a font's lines are rendered by the browser. Bold fonts use heavier lines than normal fonts, in general. A font's size is how large or small the actual individual characters are rendered by the browser.

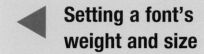

Table 14.4 CSS properties used in this task

Property	Function
font-weight	Specifies a font's weight.
font-size	Specifies a font's size.

In CSS, a font's weight is declared by the **font-weight** property. Valid values are **normal**, **bold**, **bolder**, **lighter** and **100**, **200**, **300**, **400**, **500**, **600**, **700**, **800** and **900**. The default is **normal**.

```
p {font-weight: bolder;}
p.big1 {font-weight: 900;}
p.big2 {font-weight: 500%;}
```

A font's weight is inherited from its parent element. That is, setting a **<div>** element's **font-weight** to **bold** causes paragraph elements in that **<div>** element to receive bold text also. The values **bolder** and **lighter** are relative to the parent element's font – the declaration simply instructs the browser to increase the font's weight relative to its parent's. Specifying a percentage also sets the font weight relative to its parent's. So 500% means five times the font weight of the parent element font.

Font size is declared by the **font-size** property. Valid values are **xx-small**, **x-small**, **small**, **medium**, **large**, **x-large**, **larger**, **smaller**, a percentage or **length**. The first six values (**xx-small** to **x-large**) are absolute values, as is a **length**. The **larger**, **smaller** and percentage values are relative to a parent's **font-size**. The relative length units are **em**, **ex** and **px**.

14

Setting a font's weight and size (cont.)

1. Open the HTML page from the previous task and the style.css file in your text editor, then save the HTML file with a new name.

2. Open the HTML file in your browser.

3. In the style.css file, locate the rule for the heading elements (`<h1>`, `<h2>` and so on) and add a declaration to make the font weight bold for all headings.

4. In the `<header>` rule, add a declaration to make the font size 30 point and the font weight bold.

5. Add a declaration to the footer's rule to change the font size to x-small and the font weight to bold.

6. Add a declaration to the rule for the `<dt>` element to set the font style to oblique, the font weight to bolder and the font size to larger.

```
p {font-size:16px;}
h1{font-size:2em;}
```

When no unit of length is specified, a browser assumes pixels are meant.

In this task, we will declare heavier font weights for our headings and a specific font size for our page heading to help those items stand out on the page and be clearly visible. We will reduce the size of the footer and use relative measures to enlarge some text in certain elements. The results should be obvious on the sample page, but various ways in which browsers handle the declarations can cause variance.

```
 6
 7  h1, h2, h3 {
 8    background-color: gray;
 9    color: white;
10    font-weight: bold;          3
11  }
12
13  body > footer {
14    border: 2px solid gray;
15    border-top-right-radius: 12px;
16    border-bottom-right-radius: 12px;
17    border-top-left-radius: 12px;
18    border-bottom-left-radius: 12px;
19    color: white;
20    background-color: darkgray;
21    font-size: x-small;          5
22    font-weight: bold;
23  }
24
25  body > header {
26    border-bottom-width: 5px; border-bottom-color: gray;
27    border-bottom-style: solid; border-top-width: 1px;
28    border-top-color: rgb(0,0,0); border-top-style: solid;
29    border-left-width: 1px; border-left-color: rgb(0,0,0);
30    border-left-style: solid; border-right-width: 1px;
31    border-right-color: #000000; border-right-style: solid;
32    color: white;
33    background-color: darkgray;
34    font-size: 30pt;             4
35    font-weight: bold;
36  }
37
38  dt {font-style: oblique; font-weight: bolder; font-size: larger;}    6
```

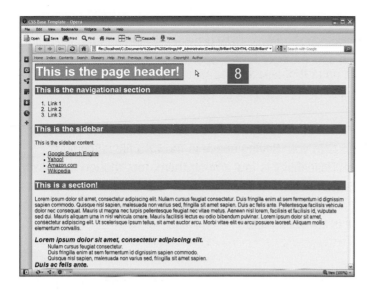

---

7 Remove the rules for the `<dl>` and `<dd>` elements.

8 Save the style sheet and refresh the web page in the browser to view the results.

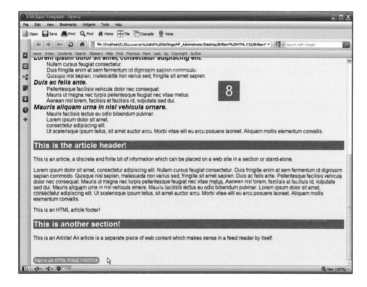

Setting font properties using the font declaration

A font's CSS properties don't need to be set singularly by separate declarations. CSS provides a single font declaration which sets multiple font properties at once.

```
p {font: normal bold 12pt Times,serif;}
```

The benefits of using a single font declaration are probably obvious to you. Saving space in the CSS file is the least of them. Readability is low among them, too, though they both offer improvements over setting properties individually. The biggest benefit, however, is efficiency. Doing more with less code is always a plus.

For your information

It may not be possible to set all font properties using a single declaration in all instances. Recall how the properties of all four border lines around the page header needed to be handled individually in order to have a single line of the border display in a different line weight. While using the convenient 'all-in-one' declaration offers efficiency, it may not be possible to do *everything* required with it alone.

The results of this task are simple and straightforward. You will replace multiple lines of CSS code with a single font declaration, saving space in the file and making the code easier to read. It may not, however, always be possible to use just a single font declaration, but it is crucial to have this option in your web design toolkit.

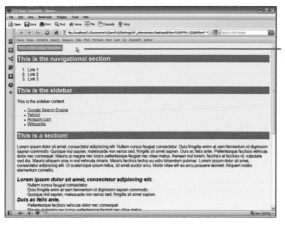

Note the reversion of the page header when font declarations are removed.

```
24
25  body > header {
26  border-bottom-width: 5px; border-bottom-color: gray;
27  border-bottom-style: solid; border-top-width: 1px;
28  border-top-color: rgb(0,0,0); border-top-style: solid;
29  border-left-width: 1px; border-left-color: rgb(0,0,0);
30  border-left-style: solid; border-right-width: 1px;
31  border-right-color: #000000; border-right-style: solid;
32  color: white;
33  background-color: darkgray;
34  font: normal bold 30pt Arial, sans-serif; ——— 4
35  }
```

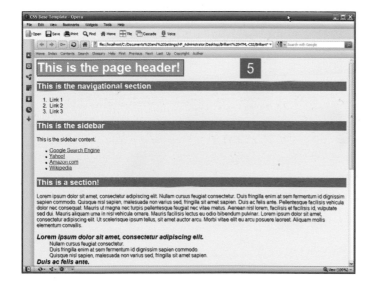

1 Open your style.css file and your sample web page in your text editor, then save the HTML file using a different name.

2 In the style sheet, locate the font declarations for the `<header>` element and remove them.

3 Save the style sheet and view the HTML page in your browser. Notice the change step 2 has made to the page header.

4 Add a single font declaration to the `<header>` element rule on the style sheet, specifying a font style of normal bold font weight, 30 point font size (30pt) and Arial font and sans-serif font family values.

5 Save the style.css file again and refresh the view in the browser.

14

Setting font properties using the font declaration (cont.)

6 Now replace the font declarations for the `<body>` element using a single font declaration of `font: normal 12pt Arial, sans-serif;}`. For the `<dt>` element, make the font style normal, font weight bold, size 13 point, font Arial and font family sans-serif (`font: normal 13pt Arial, sans-serif;`). Save the style.css file.

7 Set the `<footer>` element font declaration to normal style, bold font weight, x-small font size, Arial font and sans-serif font family (`font: normal bold x-small Arial, sans-serif;`).

8 Refresh the browser view. There should be no change to the page despite the new declarations.

```
 1
 2  body {
 3    background-color: whitesmoke;
 4    font: normal 12pt Arial, sans-serif;          6
 5  }
 6
 7  h1, h2, h3 {
 8    background-color: gray;
 9    color: white;
10    font-weight: bold;
11  }
12
13  body > footer {
14    border: 2px solid gray;
15    border-top-right-radius: 12px;
16    border-bottom-right-radius: 12px;
17    border-top-left-radius: 12px;
18    border-bottom-left-radius: 12px;
19    color: white;
20    background-color: darkgray;
21    font: normal bold x-small Arial, sans-serif;   7
22  }
23
24  body > header {
25    border-bottom-width: 5px; border-bottom-color: gray;
26    border-bottom-style: solid; border-top-width: 1px;
27    border-top-color: rgb(0,0,0); border-top-style: solid;
28    border-left-width: 1px; border-left-color: rgb(0,0,0);
29    border-left-style: solid; border-right-width: 1px;
30    border-right-color: #000000; border-right-style: solid;
31    color: white;
32    background-color: darkgray;
33    font: normal bold 30pt Arial, sans-serif;
34  }
35
36  dt {font: normal bold 13pt Arial, sans-serif;}   6
37
```

In Chapter 3 we looked at several HTML text formatting tags, but most of them, such as the `<underline>` element (`<u></u>`), have been deprecated. CSS has replaced those text formatting elements. CSS offers properties for underlining, crossing out text, making text upper case or lower case, setting initial capitals for each word and even making text blink.

Table 14.5 CSS `text-decoration` and `transform` properties

Property	Function
`text-decoration: underline`	Specifies text is underlined.
`text-decoration: overline`	Specifies text has a line above it.
`text-decoration: line-through`	Specifies text has a line through it, as if it's been crossed out. Also called strikethrough.
`text-decoration: blink`	Specifies text to blink.
`text-decoration: none`	Specifies no text decoration.
`text-transform: uppercase`	Specifies text is in upper case.
`text-transform: lowercase`	Specifies text is in lower case.
`text-transform: capitalize`	Specifies the first letter of every word is a capital.
`text-transform: none`	Specifies no text is transformed.

Not all of these properties are equally useful in all applications, of course. Line-through, where text is crossed out with a horizontal line through it, is used sort of tongue-in-cheek in many places, to show a sarcastic line replaced with a nicer one, for example but, in legal or formal documentation, it's required to show where corrections or changes have been made. How often is the overline property needed and when

Decorating text and changing case

Important

Blinking text may seem a novel idea initially, but it can be extremely annoying for someone visiting your website to have the words of a page flashing at them. The pace and position of the flashing text are critical. Use this CSS tool with caution!

14

Decorating text and changing case (cont.)

is it required? Questions about the specific content and the intended audience will offer the best guides to using text properties to good effect on a web page.

For our purposes, this task will focus on transforming lower-case text into upper-case text and making our headings stand out, as well as altering our navigational section to present itself in a more pleasing way.

Cross reference

See the task 'Aligning text' later in this chapter for more `<nav>` element formatting specifics.

The results of the task are clearly visible and our sample web page will take another step towards being fully formatted and ready for publication. As you will see in the screenshots, the page is becoming crisply delineated and professional looking. Great work so far!

For your information

Saving the HTML files isn't necessary for most of the tasks related to CSS, except where a `<style>` element is inserted on to the web page itself. It's done here to provide a way to track the completed tasks as you work through the book.

```
 7  ⊟h1, h2, h3 {
 8    background-color: gray;
 9    color: white;
10    font-weight: bold;
11    text-transform: capitalize;————— 3
12  ⌐}
13
14  ⊟body > footer {
15    border: 2px solid gray;
16    border-top-right-radius: 12px;
17    border-bottom-right-radius: 12px;
18    border-top-left-radius: 12px;
19    border-bottom-left-radius: 12px;
20    color: white;
21    background-color: darkgray;
22    font: normal bold x-small Arial, sans-serif;
23    text-transform: capitalize;————— 4
24  ⌐}
25
26  ⊟body > header {
27    border-bottom-width: 5px; border-bottom-color: gray;
28    border-bottom-style: solid; border-top-width: 1px;
29    border-top-color: rgb(0,0,0); border-top-style: solid;
30    border-left-width: 1px; border-left-color: rgb(0,0,0);
31    border-left-style: solid; border-right-width: 1px;
32    border-right-color: #000000; border-right-style: solid;
33    color: white;
34    background-color: darkgray;
35    font: normal bold 30pt Arial, sans-serif;
36    text-transform: uppercase;————— 2
37  ⌐}
38
39  ⊟body > nav {
40    background-color: black;————— 6
41    color: white;
42    text-transform: lowercase;
43  ⌐}
```

5

!

Important

Because there are other text-formatting elements, such as the `<h2>` and `<ul>` elements, within the `<nav>` element, the background may not transform. It may be necessary to remove the other formatting elements to make the changes visible, depending on how your browser handles the inheritance of element properties. For instance, in Safari, no changes are necessary in order for the changes to be made visible. Safari is the browser used to create the screenshots of the completed task.

Decorating text and changing case (cont.)

1 Open the style.css file in your text editor. If you like, open your sample web page from the previous task and save it to a new location.

2 Locate the `<header>` element's rule and add a `text-transform` declaration to set the text as all upper case (`text-transform: uppercase;`).

3 Create a declaration for the heading elements (`<h1>`, `<h2>` and so on) so the first letter of each word is changed to a capital (`text-transform: capitalize;`).

4 In the `<footer>` element rule, add the same `text-transform` declaration which you did in step 3. Make sure the HTML file's text is not all upper case or the transform may not work.

5 Add a rule to the `<nav>` element to make all the text lower case (`text-transform: lowercase;`).

14

Decorating text and changing case (cont.)

6 Make the background colour of the **<nav>** element black and the text colour white (**background-color: black; color: white;**).

7 Save the style.css file and open the HTML file in your web browser to see the results.

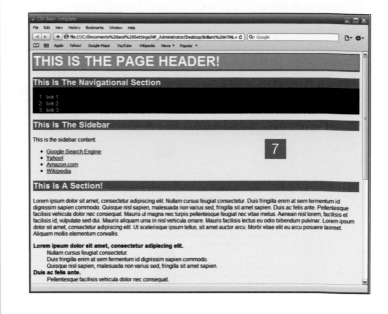

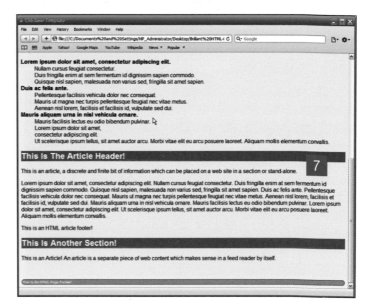

For your information

This task avoids the issue of elements within elements which can occur with the Opera™ browser, but savvy web designers address these matters. There are selectors capable of locating the correct elements no matter how deeply nested in other elements they are and formatting them.

For the purposes of this task, however, we have not delved into those selectors and combinators in order to make it straightforward.

CSS provides properties to range or align text to the left or right or justified and centre content on a page. Using text alignment to create interest can have quite an impact. As in all things, however, overindulging in such things can be problematic. Use text alignment judiciously, especially justified text (where the text is set as a block, straight down both sides, and the words spaced accordingly).

Table 14.6 CSS `text-align` properties

Property	Function
`text-align: left`	Specifies text is ranged to the left.
`text-align: right`	Specifies text is ranged to the right.
`text-align: center`	Specifies text is centred.
`text-align: justify`	Specifies text is justified.

For your information

The spacing of words on individual lines of justified text may not always be predictable. Because a browser will spread the words of a line evenly across a given space, it increases the amount of space between the words to make them fit evenly in the specified width of the block of text. You can see similar situations in word processing programs such as Microsoft Word®. A justified paragraph has straight left and right margin edges, but the spacing between the words is adjusted to achieve this. This can look particularly strange when there are only a few words or at the end of a paragraph. So, be sure to check the results before you publish a justified text.

14

Aligning text (cont.)

The outcome of the code added in this exercise is clear. The `<h2>` element text will be centred, while text in some of the other elements will be ranged right or justified. Ranging text to the left is the default for all HTML elements with Western language bases, so doesn't need to be specified.

1 Open the style.css file in your text editor. If you like, open your sample web page in your text editor, too, and save it with a new name.

2 In the style sheet, create a rule for the `<section>` element so that text will be ranged to the right (`text-align: right;`).

3 Create a rule for the `<article>` element to justify the text (`text-align: justify;`).

4 Centre the text for the `<h2>` element, but *not* the `<h1>` or `<h3>` elements. (Hint: a new rule must be created.)

5 Save the style.css file and open the HTML file in your browser to view the results.

```
13
14    h2 {text-align: center;}                              4
15
16  ⊟body > footer {
17    border: 2px solid gray;
18    border-top-right-radius: 12px;
19    border-bottom-right-radius: 12px;
20    border-top-left-radius: 12px;
21    border-bottom-left-radius: 12px;
22    color: white;
23    background-color: darkgray;
24    font: normal bold x-small Arial, sans-serif;
25    text-transform: capitalize;
26   ⌐}
27
28  ⊟body > header {
29    border-bottom-width: 5px; border-bottom-color: gray;
30    border-bottom-style: solid; border-top-width: 1px;
31    border-top-color: rgb(0,0,0); border-top-style: solid;
32    border-left-width: 1px; border-left-color: rgb(0,0,0);
33    border-left-style: solid; border-right-width: 1px;
34    border-right-color: #000000; border-right-style: solid;
35    color: white;
36    background-color: darkgray;
37    font: normal bold 30pt Arial, sans-serif;
38    text-transform: uppercase;
39   ⌐}
40
41  ⊟body nav * {
42    background-color: black;
43    color: white;
44    text-transform: lowercase;
45   ⌐}
46
47    section {text-align: right;}                          2
48
49    article {text-align: justify;}                       3
50
```

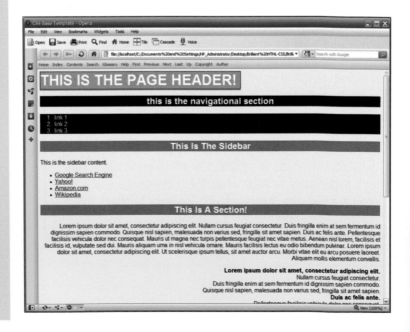

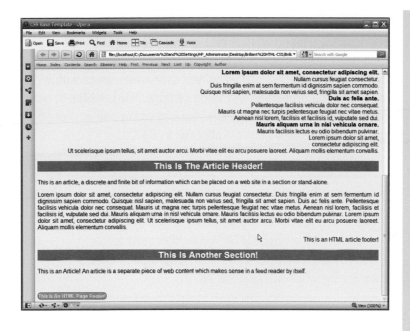

For your information

Did you notice the change to the selector for the `<nav>` element in the style sheet screenshot? It looks like this:

```
body nav * {
```

This does a couple of things, but notice how it has cleaned up the look of the `<nav>` element on the page.

First, it selects a specific `<nav>` element – the one which is the direct child of the `<body>` element. There is only a space between those selectors, so they are called 'simple selectors'. Next, the asterisk tells the browser to apply this formatting rule to *any element in the selected* `<nav>` *element*. That's key and critical! Without it, the `<nav>` element formatting would not apply to the heading element within it or to the list and list items it contains. With this combinator, however, the CSS rules apply to the elements chosen without having to select each one individually.

14

Formatting text using word and letter spacing

One important factor in web design which it's easy to overlook is white space. Having white space makes it easier to read content on a page (web or print), avoiding it looking overcrowded and hard to navigate. CSS allows control over white space with a large array of properties and value settings. It's possible to get exactly the look and feel the site requires using one or more of the text white space controls afforded in CSS.

Cross reference

See the quick reference guide for CSS3 you downloaded previously (at: **www.veign.com**) for a complete list of the text controls available in CSS, including white space controls.

This task focuses on the easy to control – and visually obvious – white space manipulators in an experimental way only. We will not be using these to insert additional white space into our content, but it does allow us to demonstrate, on an exaggerated scale, how white space can be controlled on a web page to affect the look and feel of the content. Once the task has been completed, we'll restore the sample web page to its previous state for future tasks.

Table 14.7 CSS word- and letter-spacing properties

Property	Function
word-spacing	Specifies space added between words.
letter-spacing	Specifies space added between letters.
text-indent	Specifies size of the indent for text.

```
45 }
46
47  section {text-align: right; word-spacing: 15pt;}
48
49  article {text-align: justify;}
```

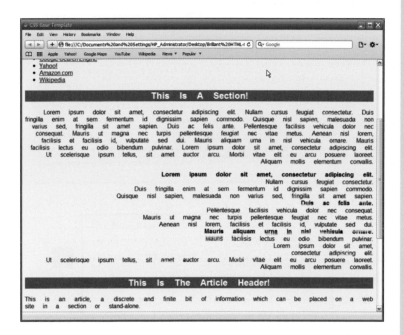

```
46
47  section {
48  text-align: right;
49  letter-spacing: 6pt; ——————— 4
50  }
51
52  article {text-align: justify;}
```

Formatting text using word and letter spacing (cont.)

1. Open the style.css file in your text editor and, if you like, open your sample web page, too, and save it with a new name.

2. In the `<section>` element rule, add a word spacing declaration so the words will be spaced apart by 15 points (there will be 15 point font-sized spaces between each word) to create additional white space (`word-spacing: 15pt;`).

3. Save the style sheet and open the HTML file in your web browser to view the results.

4. Edit the CSS rule for the `<section>` element so the letter spacing will be increased to 6 points (`letter-spacing: 6pt;`).

14

Formatting text using word and letter spacing (cont.)

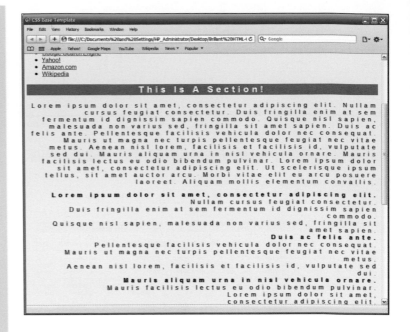

5 Save the style sheet and refresh the web page in your browser to view the results.

6 Remove the letter spacing property from the `<section>` element and set the alignment for the `<article>` element text to 'justify' (`text-align: justify;`).

7 Also add a declaration to the `<article>` rule to indent the text by 20 pixels (`text-indent: 20px;`).

8 Save the style.css file and refresh the page in your browser to view the results.

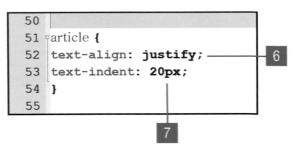

```
50
51  article {
52    text-align: justify;      6
53    text-indent: 20px;
54  }
55
```

7

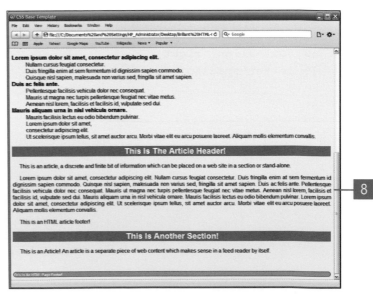

8

For your information

A paragraph's wrapping behaviour can be set using the CSS **white-space** property. Valid values are **normal**, **pre** and **nowrap**. For example:

```
p {white-space: nowrap;}
```

Specifying **pre** preserves all white space. This property's behaviour is the same as the HTML <pre> tag. Specifying **nowrap** prevents text wrapping, but a long line forces readers to scroll horizontally to read it, which they may not like.

14

Adding drop shadows to text

Most often, adding special effects to text content requires the content to be manipulated in a graphics or photo editing program, such as Adobe Photoshop® and then placed on a web page as an image. CSS3 changes the game, however, and has some wonderful special effects which can be applied to text to achieve stunning visual properties without the expense or learning curve required to use photo-editing software.

One of the new special effects available in CSS3 is the text shadow, which creates a three-dimensional effect by adding a drop shadow behind the text content on the screen. Depending on the colour, diffusion (or spread) and distance from the text, wonderful effects can be achieved. It's even possible to make text appear as though it's aflame.

As with many other aspects of CSS, however, special effects must be used prudently. In the following task, our web page will include only one, though others are and will be available as more of the recommendation document for CSS3 is incorporated into browser's standards.

Table 14.8 CSS `text-shadow` property

Property	Function
text-shadow	Specifies the distance down and to the right of the text the shadow is to extend. It requires a colour for the shadow be indicated, by hexadecimal number or name.

It is a simple and easy task, but has great impact. A drop shadow will appear under the text of the `<dt>` element, 5 pixels below and to the right, diffused by 5 pixels as well. A hexadecimal value of a grey (#666) is used which is not so dark that you can't read the text on top of it and not so light that you'll fail to notice it on the page.

Cross reference

See the work of the amazing and talented web designers at **www.catswhocode.com** for some fantastic ideas and explanations of how to use the exciting features of CSS3 to create effects formerly only available to Adobe Photoshop® artists.

```
56 dt {
57 font: normal bold 13pt Arial, sans-serif;
58 text-shadow: 5px 5px 5px #666; ——— 2
59 }
60
```

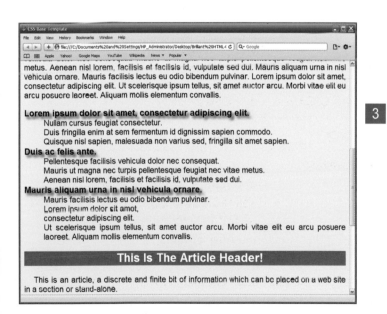

Adding drop shadows to text (cont.)

1 Open your style.css file in your text editor and, if you like, open the HTML file from the last task and save it with a new name.

2 Locate the `<dt>` rule in the style sheet and add a declaration for a drop shadow with a drop of 5 pixels, a right offset of 5 pixels, and a spread of 5 pixels. Use the colour #666 for the final part of the declaration (`text-shadow: 5px 5px 5px #666;`).

3 Save the style sheet and load the HTML file in your web browser to view the result.

4 Experiment with the offset distances and the colours to find interesting and exciting combinations.

14

CSS margins, padding and element size

15

Introduction

If you've worked sequentially through this book's chapters and tasks, you will already have worked with CSS borders. Essentially, borders are the boundaries or lines around the edges of the elements on your web page. All structural elements have borders, including paragraph `<p>` elements. In the context of this chapter's discussion, however, borders have another use which has nothing to do with aesthetics and everything to do with position and page white space (as opposed to white space between words and letters of specific content).

In Chapter 6, you learned about cell margins, borders and padding. Those things work the same way for HTML elements as they did for HTML tables and, in fact, you can think of elements on a web page as cells of a sort. The term 'border' here refers to the edge or boundary of an element, while 'padding' refers to the space between the content of an element and its border. 'Margin' refers to the space between elements on a page.

Envisioning the elements on a web page as boxes composed of borders, margins and padding is referred to as the 'box model' in CSS. Specific elements can be positioned on a page with precision to create a logical, natural content flow.

Because borders were covered in Chapter 12, here the focus will be on margins and padding, with the aim of cleaning up our sample web page visually and making it easier to read and more professional in appearance.

An element's internal padding – the space between the

What you'll do

Set an element's padding

Set an element's margins

Set relative width and height

Set absolute width and height

Cross reference

See Chapter 16 for more information on positioning HTML elements using CSS properties.

Cross reference

See Chapter 12, 'Setting borders with CSS', for more details on working with CSS borders.

Setting an element's padding

element's content and its border – is set by the CSS **padding** property. For example:

```
p {padding: 5px;}
```

assigns a 5-pixel space (padding) between the paragraph's text and border.

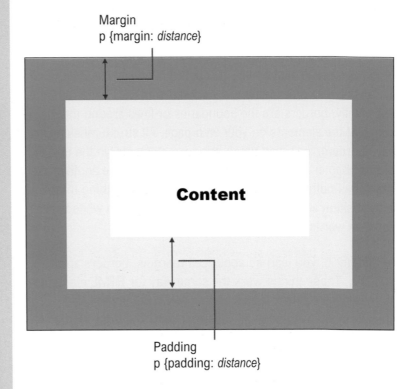

Margin
p {margin: *distance*}

Content

Padding
p {padding: *distance*}

To set padding, the top, bottom, left and right padding amounts are coded individually as separate declarations:

```
p {
padding-top:2px;
padding-bottom:3px;
padding-left:3px;
padding-right:4px;
}
```

in a single declaration:

```
p {padding: 2px 3px 3px 4px;}
```

or, if the values are the same for all sides, all four properties can be set by one value:

```
p {padding:4px;}
```

Table 15.1 CSS `padding` properties

Property	Function
`padding-top`	Specifies the padding at the top of an element.
`padding-right`	Specifies the padding to the right of an element.
`padding-bottom`	Specifies the padding at the bottom of an element.
`padding-left`	Specifies the padding to the left of an element.
`padding`	Specifies all four sides of an element's padding in a single statement.

The results of this task are visible but may not be obvious initially. When the separate declarations are used to set the padding of the `<nav>` element, the text is moved in from the edge by 10 pixels. To make this more obvious, you could use an exaggerated figure, such as 50px or 100px, to see clearly how the impact is made.

Additionally, we will change the single declaration to two separate `padding-right` and `padding-left` declarations. Alternatively, we could use 0px as the values for the top and bottom padding for the element (or a smaller value, such as 2px). When using the single `padding` declaration, the order of sides is top, right, bottom, left (`padding: topvalue rightvalue bottomvalue leftvalue`). So, a single declaration with 2px of padding at the top and bottom and 20px at the left and right would read: `padding: 2px 20px 2px 20px;`. Again, the more efficient the code, the better and more legible it will be.

Setting an element's padding (cont.)

1 Open the HTML file you created from the previous chapter in your text editor and save it with a new name, then launch the file in your web browser.

2 In the browser, notice the spaces between the content and borders on the page. The `<nav>` element is probably the clearest example of this.

3 Open the style.css file in your text editor.

4 Locate the `<nav>` element and type a declaration to add 10 pixels' padding to this element (`padding: 10px 10px 10px 10px;`)

For your information

You may be wondering why legibility of code is important. For one thing, you may need to edit the code at some future point and being able to decipher what you did is critical (although not such a major consideration with CSS as its syntax is fairly intuitive). Also, another web designer may be required to pick up where a previous one left off. If you're the successor to an earlier designer, it's certain you'll appreciate having code clearly annotated with comments and easy to read visually. Doing the same yourself is a 'best practice' – a good habit to form and utilise.

```
40
41 body nav * {
42 background-color: black;
43 color: white;
44 text-transform: lowercase;
45 padding-left: 10px;
46 padding-right: 10px;            4
47 }
48
```

! **Important**

! **Important**

As with other selectors, combinators can be used instead to format *only* the precise elements targeted. If you're interested in finding out about those combinators and selectors, consult the quick reference guide you downloaded before (at: **www.veign.com**) or from any online CSS3 resource for more information.

7

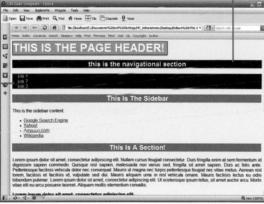

Note the change in this distance.

5 Save the file and refresh the browser view to see the results.

6 Notice the padding has been added to all the elements in the **<nav>** element, including the **<h2>** element. Change the padding declaration from a single statement to two separate declarations for the left and right padding to be 10 pixels (**padding-left: 10px; padding-right: 10px;**).

7 Save the style sheet and refresh the page in the browser again and view the results.

15

Setting an element's margins

A margin is the space between elements. It's a cushion around an element's border which no other elements may intrude on. For instance, if two elements have a 5-pixel margin, the total space between them would be 10 pixels.

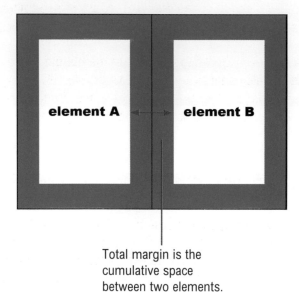

Total margin is the cumulative space between two elements.

Elements each have a right, left, top and bottom margin. Margins – just like padding and many other CSS properties – can be set either separately or together in one declaration. A margin's width may be a length (in pixels), a percentage or auto. As with other elements, length is a fixed measurement and percentage refers to the margin's parent element. Auto allows the *browser* to determine the margin.

Table 15.2 CSS `margin` properties

Property	Function
`margin-right`	Specifies an element's right-hand margin.
`margin-left`	Specifies an element's left-hand margin.
`margin-top`	Specifies an element's top margin.
`margin-bottom`	Specifies an element's bottom margin.
`margin`	Specifies an element's margin.

Margins can be eliminated to butt adjacent elements together or else increased to add white space to the overall page. The desired effect will determine whether you increase or decrease margins, just as it does with padding. It may also be necessary to increase padding in one area and reduce it on another side to create the desired look.

In this task, we will eliminate some of the margin space around our elements to achieve a crisper look. If the page now feels 'cluttered' or busy, increase either the padding or margins to create the look and feel of the page you want.

For your information

Remember, we open and save the HTML file strictly for tracking purposes. There is no need to alter the HTML file in any way, but, by saving with a new name, you can track your progress through the chapters. You could save the style.css file with a new name (it must still have the .css file extension), but, if you do that, you need to update the **<link>** element's **href** property to reflect the new name.

```
13
14  h2 {
15  text-align: center;
16  margin: 5px 0px 0px 0px
17  }
18
```
2

1 Open the style.css file in your text editor and, if you like, open the sample web page from the previous task, too, and save it with a new name.

2 Locate the **<h2>** rule in the style sheet. Edit the rule to eliminate the margin space on the right, left and bottom, while setting the top margin to 5 pixels (**margin: 5px 0px 0px 0px;**).

3 Save the style.css file. Refresh the sample page in the browser and view the results.

15

Setting an element's margins (cont.)

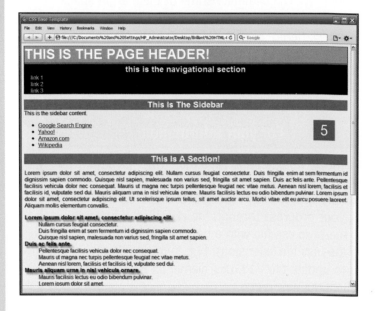

```
42
43  body nav * {
44  background-color: black; color: white;
45  text-transform: lowercase;
46  padding-left: 10px; padding-right: 10px;
47  margin-top: 0px; ——— 4
48  }
49
```

4 Find the rule for the `<nav>` element and add a declaration to eliminate the top margin space (`margin-top: 0px;`).

5 Save the style sheet again and refresh the browser view to see the effects of your changes.

For your information

At this juncture, the page header won't display correctly in all browsers. Consider the screenshot below from the Opera™ browser, for instance.

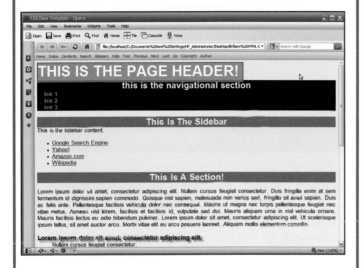

As you can see, the `<header>` element doesn't display across the entire page width as the other heading elements do. That is because different browsers interpret the CSS rules differently. Compare the Opera™ browser's version with the display from Safari in the screenshot for step 5 opposite. Safari's handling of the `<header>` element is much more in keeping with the intended design.

If a browser doesn't display the design you've created properly, don't despair. Many such problems can be overcome with relative ease with just a bit more diligence and code work. We can address the `<header>` element here, for example, by adding the following declaration to the `<header>` rule: `display: block;`. It causes the element to display as a block element, meaning that a line break is created before and after the element, so it is alone on the line. This corrects Opera™'s display problem. Add the line to the rule if you like and you're using Opera™.

15

Setting relative width and height

An element's width and height are declared by the `width` and `height` properties. Both allow values of `auto`, a `length` in pixels or a percentage relative to the parent element.

Clearly, an element's width and height can have a major impact on a page's layout. When setting a relative width and height, the size of the element is determined in relation to its parent. For example, if a `<div>` element with a width 50 per cent of the page width contains a `<p>` element set to 50 per cent in its `width` property, then the `<p>` width is 50 per cent of the parent element and 25 per cent of the page width.

For your information

If you find the concept of relative sizing is confusing, think about it this way: the size setting for any element (`height` or `width` or both) is relative to the container holding it. If the element takes up half the container, its size depends on the size of the container holding it, so 50 per cent in `height` and `width` settings can be very large or very small, depending on how large or small the container is. Rather like goldfish in a bowl, the elements expand to fill the space they're afforded. Unlike goldfish, however, they will shrink to accommodate reductions in container sizes, too.

Absolute length values define height and width regardless of the parent element's settings. Moreover, as the browser window is resized, elements with relative width and height settings resize themselves in relation to the browser. Elements with a fixed height and width do not.

This task will enable us to create a bit of white space around the edges of our page and give us the opportunity to position and size our elements relative to the window in which they'll be displayed. The results of the task code will become most evident when the browser window is adjusted and resized and the sample page adjusts with it.

```
1
2  body {
3  background-color: whitesmoke;
4  font: normal 12pt Arial, sans-serif;
5  width: 90%; margin-left: 5%;
6  }
7
```

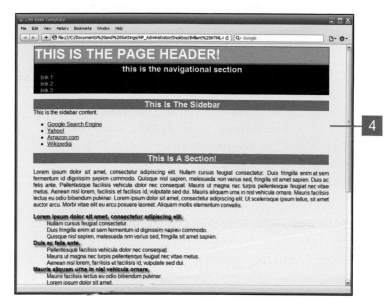

1 Open the style.css file in your text editor and, if you like, open the HTML file used in the previous task and save it with a new name.

2 In the style sheet, locate the rule for the <body> element. Add a declaration to reduce the size of the body element to 85 per cent relative to the containing element's width – in this case, the containing element is the <html> element (width: 90%;).

3 In order to keep the <body> element centred on the page (its default position is ranged left), set the left margin to half of the remaining screen width (margin-left: 5%;).

4 Open the HTML file in your web browser to view the results. As an experiment, try resizing the browser window to several different shapes and watch the content adjust to maintain the settings coded.

15

Setting absolute width and height

In the last task the `<body>` element's width and height were relative to those of its parent (which is the `<html>` element). When the page's dimensions changed, because of the relative percentages used for values, the `<body>` element adjusted its size accordingly.

When using a fixed measurement for these settings, an element's width and height are no longer in relation to its parent's dimensions. Instead the element is sized precisely to a specified `width` and `height` and remains that size.

1. Open the style.css file in your text editor. If you like, open the HTML file, too, and save it with a new name.

2. In the style sheet, edit the `<body>` element rule to change the dimensions from 90 per cent of the parent element to a fixed size of 960px.

```
1
2  body {
3    background-color: whitesmoke;
4    font: normal 12pt Arial, sans-serif;
5    width: 960px; margin-left: 5%;
6  }
7
```

3. Save the style sheet and open the HTML file in your browser to view the results. Adjust the window and see the page doesn't resize to accommodate it.

4. In the style sheet, edit the `<body>` element dimensions again, this time setting them to 700px, and save the style sheet once again.

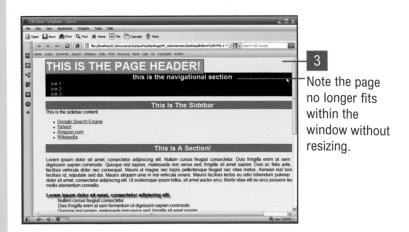

Note the page no longer fits within the window without resizing.

```
1
2  body {
3    background-color: whitesmoke;
4    font: normal 12pt Arial, sans-serif;
5    width: 700px; margin-left: 5%;
6  }
7
```

4

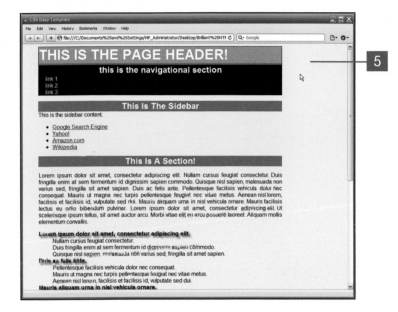

5

5 Refresh the view in the browser to view the results. Experiment with different window sizes and notice how the page does not adjust to the window any longer.

6 Edit the `<body>` element dimensions so they are again 90 per cent relative to the parent element and save the style sheet.

Cross reference

There are many other position and sizing elements available to web designers which make it possible to establish elements on a page with extreme precision. Check out CSS3 design sites and tutorials for more information.

15

Positioning elements using CSS

Introduction

Part of ensuring a web page will have the look and feel desired is checking the elements are correctly positioned. If you're using a tool such as Adobe Dreamweaver® or a similar web development tool, you may have a drag and drop facility, but, for true control and understanding of how to position an element, CSS is the tool to use.

Unless specifically instructed otherwise, a browser will position elements as they appear in the HTML file for the page. That is, they'll be positioned as the browser encounters them. Block-level elements – content in 'block' groupings, separate from other content, such as the `<h1>` to `<h6>` elements – are placed, top to bottom, on their own line(s) as they're read by the browser. Inline elements – the position of the content is maintained while it's being formatted, such as the `<b>` or `<i>` tags – are placed left to right on the lines in which they appear.

In short, a browser reads and displays elements top-to-bottom and left-to-right, unless instructed otherwise by CSS code.

CSS provides instructions to position elements in absolute, relative or fixed positions and, for positioning elements, beside other elements. Recall from Chapter 15, CSS's 'block model', wherein elements are considered in terms of being blocks on a page. Those blocks are what is positioned on the web page. Sometimes, elements which may not be block elements can be displayed as block elements using CSS.

What you'll do

Position elements with `float` and `clear`

Absolute positioning of elements

Relative positioning of elements

Fixed positioning of elements

Layer elements using CSS

Using the tools CSS supplies, in this chapter, we will position some of the block elements on our sample web page and turn our navigational section into a more traditional link arrangement. When you've completed these tasks, your sample web page will be ready for actual content and publication on a web hosting service.

The **float** property moves an element as far to the right or left as possible within the element's parent. Other normal-flowing elements flow *around* the floated element, to its right or left.

Specifying **float:right** instructs browsers to place other elements on the floated element's left. Specifying **float:left** places elements on the floated element's right. In this way, it's possible to position a picture precisely within content or a structural element. For instance, an image may float left of a paragraph with **float:left**. To float the image to the right side, use **float:right**.

The **clear** property specifies an element may not have another element float to its left or right or both.

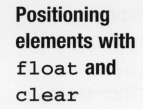

Table 16.1 CSS **float** and **clear** property value settings

Property	Function
float	Specifies an element should be placed to one side or the other of all other normal-flowing elements.
Left	Specifies an element float to the left of other normal-flowing elements.
Right	Specifies an element float to the right of other normal-flowing elements.
None	Specifies an element does not float.
Inherit	Specifies an element inherit its containing ancestor's float value.
clear	Specifies one or both sides to which other floated elements may not be set.
Both	Specifies floated elements may not float to either the left or right of an element.
left	Specifies no floated elements may float to the left of an element.
right	Specifies no floated element may float to the right of an element.
none	Allows elements to float to the left or right or both sides of an element.
inherit	Specifies the block-level element inherits its containing ancestor's clear value.

Positioning elements with `float` and `clear` (cont.)

1. Open the sample web page you created in the last chapter in your web browser. If you like, open the HTML file in your text editor and save it with a new name.

2. Open the style.css file in your text editor.

3. In the rule for the page header, add the `clear` property, set to the value `both`.

4. Add a rule for the `<aside>` element, with the `float` set to `right`. To increase its visibility, add a `margin` setting of 20px to the element's bottom and left sides.

5. Add a declaration to the rule to set the `padding` to 20px on both sides and the bottom of the element (with 0px on the top). Also, set a border of 2px in a dashed style with a colour value of black, change the background colour to 'darkgray' and set the font colour to 'black'.

The results of this task should be obvious and clear immediately. Once the `<aside>` element has been positioned and sized, it should appear to the right side of the page. We will use the `float` property to put the element all the way to the right of the page.

```
60  aside {
61    float:right;                          4
62    margin: 0px 0px 20px 20px;
63    padding: 0px 20px 20px 20px;
64    border: 2px dashed black;            5
65    background-color: darkgray;
66    color: black;
67  }
68
69  aside > h2 {
70    background-color: darkgray;
71    color: black;                        6
72    padding: 0;
73    margin: 0;
74  }
75
```

For your information

There are myriad ways to accomplish the task of setting the sidebar apart. Along with positioning the element with `float` and `clear` properties, the `display` property and `vertical-alignment` property can be set to create a standalone sidebar element.

6 Create a new rule for an `<h2>` element within the `<aside>` element. Set the background colour to 'darkgray', the foreground colour to 'black', and both the padding and margin to 0.

7 Save the style sheet and refresh the browser view to see the results.

8 As an optional step, add the `clear` property to the `<nav>` element rule with a value set to 'both'.

Important

Remember to use combinators to create specific selectors. This will be a skill of great use to you in web design.

Absolute positioning of elements

In the CSS box model of a normal-flowing page layout, elements are positioned as blocks wherever they appear in the code. With absolute positioning, however, the browser is *instructed* where to place the element on the page, regardless of other factors, including normal page flow. The element is removed from the page flow in favour of its position being stated specifically.

Four properties are used to establish elements' positions: `top`, `right`, `bottom` and `left`. The `top` property declares how far from the top of the page the browser is to place the top edge of our element. Positive values move the element *down* the page; negative values move the element *up* the page.

The `right` property determines how far from the right edge of the page the right edge of the element is to be placed, while the `left` property determines how far from the edge of the left side of the page to position the left edge of the element edge. The `bottom` property determines how far from the bottom of the page's edge to place the element's bottom edge.

Table 16.2 Absolute positioning property and offsets

Property	Function
`position: absolute`	Specifies the absolute positioning of an element on a web page.
`top`	Specifies the distance from an element's top edge to the containing element's top edge.
`right`	Specifies the distance from the element's right edge to the containing element's right edge.
`left`	Specifies the distance from the element's left edge to the containing element's left edge.
`bottom`	Specifies the distance from the element's bottom edge to the containing element's bottom edge.

For your information

The units for the values are set in either CSS units, which are pixels (px), font size-relative – that is, ems, where 1 em is the current font size – or centimetres (cm). The values can also be set in percentages (%) of the parent element's dimensions.

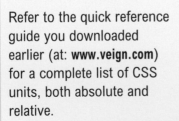

Cross reference

Refer to the quick reference guide you downloaded earlier (at: **www.veign.com**) for a complete list of CSS units, both absolute and relative.

When the four corners of the parent element are considered as '0' points for the positioning of the elements they contain, the absolute positioning system becomes clear, even intuitive.

In this task, we will add an image to the sample web page and position it on the page with absolute settings. The position of the image will be unaffected by moving the code around in the element. Resizing the window does not alter where the image is placed either. In fact, the image may not even be within the confines of the element in which it's placed as, for absolute positioning, the parent element is the **<body>** element and the '0' points are the corners of the web browser's window, *not* the corners of the **<article>** element in which the image is initially placed.

Absolute positioning of elements (cont.)

16

1. Open the sample web page from the previous task in your text editor and save it with a new name.

2. Locate an image you can add to the web page and save or copy it to the same folder you just saved the HTML file to.

3. In the first **<article>** element, insert the image using the **<img>** tag below the article's heading.

> ### Important !
>
> As a reminder, it is *not* permissible to use just any image gathered from the Internet. Before using an image, either obtain permission from the owner of it or be sure to use images with no copyright entanglements.

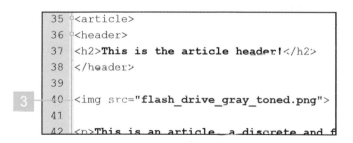

```
35  <article>
36  <header>
37  <h2>This is the article header!</h2>
38  </header>
39
40  <img src="flash_drive_gray_toned.png">
41
42  <p>This is an article, a discrete and f
```

Absolute positioning of elements (cont.)

Cross reference

See Chapter 5 for more information on working with the `<img>` tag.

4. Save the HTML file and open it in your web browser to see the normal position of the image as determined by the browser.

5. Open the style.css file in your text editor.

6. Create a rule for an `<img>` tag in an `<article>` element which assigns an absolute position for the image of right by 200 pixels and moves the top down by 20 per cent (`position: absolute; left: 200px; top: 20%;`).

7. Save the style sheet and refresh the browser view to see the results.

8. As an experiment, resize the window several times and in different ways to see how this impacts the positioning of the image on the page.

```
54
55  img {
56    position: absolute; left: 200px; top: 20%;
57  }
58
```

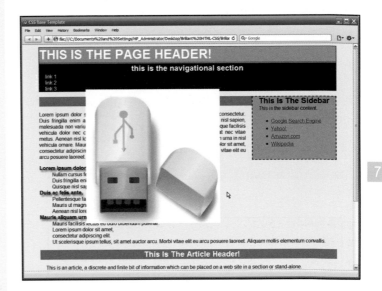

Relative positioning allows elements to be positioned relative to their normal positions, as determined by a browser.

Relative positioning specifies how many pixels left, right, above or below an element's normal position it will be placed using the **left**, **right**, **top** and **bottom** offsets. For instance, an image can be placed 15 pixels down and 10 pixels right of its normal position as follows:

```
img {position: relative; left: 10px;
top: 15px;}
```

This declaration means the image is being placed with its left edge 10 pixels to the right and its top edge 15 pixels down. To move the image to the left, we'd specify the position as:

```
img {position: relative; right: 10px;
top: 15px;}
```

This declaration moves the image's right edge 10 pixels to the left rather than the right.

Relative positioning of elements

For your information

You could use a negative number for the value of the **left** property in the first example of code to have a similar effect to that of using the **right** property in the second line of code. That is, you would enter:

```
{position: relative; left: -10px;}
```

Relative positioning of elements (cont.)

1. Open the sample web page from the previous task in your text editor and save it with a new name.

2. Open the style.css file in your text editor.

3. Edit the rule for the `<img>` tag to place the image to the right relative to its normal position by 200 pixels and the top down from its normal position by 1 per cent. **(position: relative; left: 200px; top: 1%;)**.

Table 16.3 Relative positioning property and offsets

Property	Function
`position: relative`	Specifies an element is positioned relative to its normal position by a browser.
`left`	Specifies an element is positioned to the right of its normal position.
`right`	Specifies an element is positioned to the left of its normal position.
`top`	Specifies an element is positioned down from its normal position.
`bottom`	Specifies an element is positioned up from its normal position.

In this task, an image will be positioned on the sample page with measures relative to the containing element. The difference between absolute and relative positioning will then become very clear.

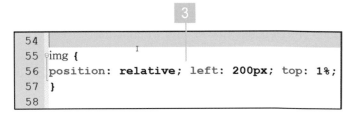

```
54
55  img {
56  position: relative; left: 200px; top: 1%;
57  }
58
```

4

4 Save the style sheet and refresh the browser view to see the results.

Fixed positioning of elements

Fixed positioning is similar to absolute positioning, except that the position is fixed relative to the browser window. The parent container is irrelevant in this case. The element remains in its fixed position relative to the browser window regardless of its size. Scrolling has no effect on the element either – it remains in one spot as the rest of the content scrolls. Absolute positioning offsets are identical to fixed positioning offsets. The only difference is that the offset is in relation to the browser's viewpoint rather than that of the entire page.

1. Open the HTML file you used in the last example in your text editor and save it with a new name.

2. If the `<img>` tag isn't there for some reason, add it per the instructions in step 3 of the task Absolute positioning of elements, page 257.

3. Open the style.css file in your text editor and edit the rule for the `<img>` tag so the image is now in a fixed position, which is the same location as currently stated.

Table 16.4 Fixed positioning property and offsets

Property	Function
`position: fixed`	Specifies an element's position is fixed relative to the browser window. The position is not impacted by scrolling or window size changes.
`left`	Specifies an element is positioned to the right of its normal position.
`right`	Specifies an element is positioned to the left of its normal position.
`top`	Specifies an element is positioned down from its normal position.
`bottom`	Specifies an element is positioned up from its normal position.

```
54
55  img {
56  position: fixed; left: 200px; top: 1%;
57  }
58
59  dt {
```

Timesaver tip

Just change the word 'relative' to 'fixed' in your style sheet to edit the rule in step 3 above.

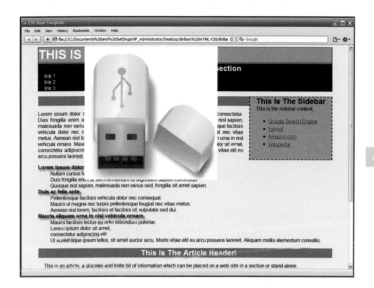

4 Save the style sheet and open the HTML file in your web browser to view the results.

5 Resize the window several times to see the impact of the changes on the image. Also, see if scrolling affects the position of the image in the browser window.

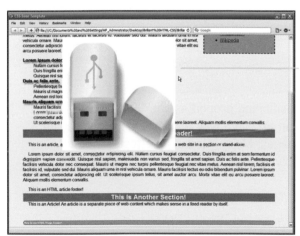

Scrolling has no effect on the image's position in the browser window.

Layering elements using CSS

▶

Positioning elements on a page or within a containing element is fine, but CSS is capable of much more.

Positioning an element on a page and partially in front of other elements is called 'layering' the content. With CSS, layers of content can be used to create interesting and dramatic effects on web pages.

Table 16.5 The `z-index` property

Property	Function
z-index	Specifies the layering level of an element. The values are `auto`, which uses the same layer level as the parent element, and an integer. The higher the integer, the higher up the stack the element is layered.

With the `z-index` property, setting the value to `auto` instructs the element to maintain the parent element's layer level. Higher levels are set by using higher integers to raise the layering level or lower integers to lower the layer level. Therefore, a `z-index` of 1 positions an element under an element with a `z-index` of 2.

ⓘ

For your information

Combining positioning properties with `z-index` properties is an excellent way to create visually pleasing, diverse web pages. Many interesting effects can be achieved simply by layering content and images on a static page.

```
54
55  img {
56    position: absolute; left: 200px; top: 1%;
57    z-index: -1;
58  }
59
```

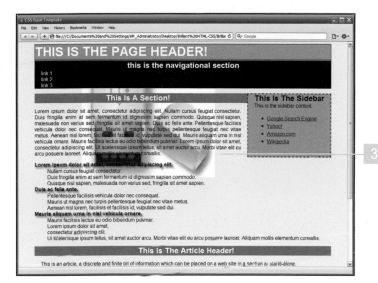

1. Open the sample web page from the previous task in your text editor and save it with a new name.

2. Locate the rule for the `<img>` tag and edit it to set the `z-index` to −1. Also, set the positioning from 'fixed' back to 'absolute'.

3. Save the style sheet and open the HTML file in your web browser to view the results. Note how the image has moved to behind the other content.

Some final thoughts on CSS

Introduction

When I sat down to write this chapter, I had a couple of tough choices to make. This book is about HTML5 and how to use it to create web pages and structure them. It's also about CSS3, which provides many interesting and dynamic ways to format HTML pages. Like most other books of this size, however, it's not a completely comprehensive discussion of all the aspects of the technology. Rather, it's a starting point to give you just what you need to know and how to do it. Along with the specifics of CSS, I have tried to give you some indication of where to go for more information. With CSS3, that's generally the W3C (at: **www.w3.org**) or CSS3.info (at: **www.css3.info**), which are both terrific sources of information.

Eventually, though, I had to decide what is critical when learning to code using CSS and what isn't, just as I had to with HTML, so some things have been left out. Nevertheless, the tools and information for expanding on what you've learned in the course of this book are now in your hands and can be used and developed as you desire, in any direction, with confidence.

That being said, the few remaining tasks this chapter offers are designed to polish up our sample web page, make it look a bit more professional and prepare it for publication on the Internet, if you so choose. In them you'll find a few tips and tricks which you can use as you move forward in your web designing future.

What you'll do

Create a navigation bar from an ordered list

Set sidebar properties

Clean up text and add white space

For your information

Don't worry – just because I haven't mentioned certain features of CSS3 doesn't mean you can't still learn about them from the source(s). Be sure to check with the latest CSS3 recommendation documents (at: **www. w3.org**) to find out what's new and cool. Also, don't underestimate the power of searching for new CSS3 information using your favourite search engine – you'll be amazed how much you can turn up.

Creating a navigation bar from an ordered list

It makes sense to address our HTML file from the sample web page from top to bottom, as that's how it's read by the browser and it's what the eyes of visitors will see. So, let's tackle the navigation bar first and make it look more like a traditional navigation bar without giving up on our unordered list (`<ul>...</ul>`) and list item (`<li>...</li>`) tags.

For your information

We could easily replace the unordered list with a single-row table which houses our links in a neat and orderly way horizontally, but the skills learned doing this task can be applied to other areas of web design and are worth knowing. Always be aware, though, whatever method you choose, an alternative is probably available and may be easier and simpler than the solution which first comes to mind.

You can accomplish a great deal with an unordered list and its associated list item tags. In this task, we will change the list so it runs horizontally rather than vertically, setting our links (which aren't active links, incidentally) across the `<nav>` section in a link bar.

Cross reference

See the quick reference guide you downloaded earlier (at: **www.veign.com**) for more information and values for the `display` property used in this task.

Table 17.1 CSS property used in this task

Property	Function
display	Specifies how to display an element. There are many choices, including **block**, which displays the element with a line break before and after it as a block-level element, and **inline**, which does not include a line break before and after the element and displays it as an inline element.

In this task, we will practise using **margin** and **padding** declarations to adjust the distance between elements and content on our page. We will use the **display: inline** property declaration to display the **<li>** elements inline – that is, the list items appear side by side on the page rather than being stacked vertically in the usual format.

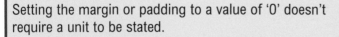

```
43
44  body nav * {
45  background-color: black; color: white;
46  text-transform: lowercase;
47  padding: 3px 10px 3px 10px;      5
48  margin: 0 auto;
49  font: normal bold 14pt Arial,sans-serif;   6
50  }
51
52  ol > li {
53  display: inline;      7
54  }
55
```
4

Timesaver tip

Setting the margin or padding to a value of '0' doesn't require a unit to be stated.

Creating a navigation bar from an ordered list (cont.)

17

1 Open the HTML file you saved in the last task of the previous chapter in your text editor and save it with a new name.

2 Remove the **<h2>** element and its content from the **<nav>** element, leaving only the **<ol>** and **<li>** elements in place. Save the HTML file again.

3 Open the style.css file in your text editor and locate the **<nav>** element rule.

4 In the **<nav>** rule, add a declaration which sets the margin to 0 for the top and a value of 'auto' for the other three sides.

5 Add another declaration which sets the padding to 3px on the top and bottom and 10px on both sides.

6 If the font isn't set correctly, make a declaration which sets it to normal style, bold weight, 14-pt size and Arial font, sans serif font family.

7 Add a rule for the **<li>** tags which follow the **<ol>** tag (that is, use the 'greater than' – > – combinator: **ol > li**) to set the **float** property to 'inline'.

Creating a navigation bar from an ordered list (cont.)

8 Locate the `<h2>` element rule and set the margins to '0' for the top and 'auto' for all the sides.

9 Save the style sheet and open the new HTML file in your browser to view the results.

Timesaver tip

Use a single declaration to set all the values for a property whenever it's practical to do so. In step 5, the padding setting is `padding: 3px 10px 3px 10px;`. If the margins declaration was `margin: 5px;`, it would set all four sides to the single value declared.

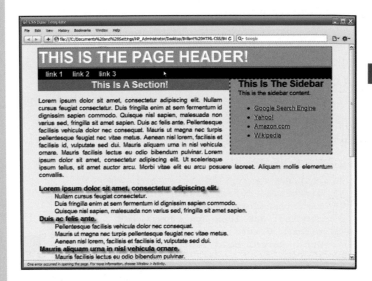

9

Next, let's address our sidebar. It's in the right place – thanks to the `float` property we used previously – but the dashed border doesn't look very nice and really isn't necessary if we can just get the setup correct. In fact, the font's too large and the heading could do with being be adjusted, too. We'll take care of all of that next.

In Chapter 15, you may recall, we discussed the use of white space to increase readability and clarity of the content on a web page. In this task we'll expand a bit on what we did and, rather than just focus on padding and margins – that is, the white space between elements – we'll increase the space between the lines of text using the `line-height` property, which will open the page up a bit. The amount of visual space we create in so doing will help to make the content in the sidebar easier to read.

We'll adjust the font in the sidebar and make it a bit smaller to help it recede into the background just a touch, which will also help the main page's content to stand out. We'll use the value unit **em**, based on current font size, to adjust the font in the sidebar.

For your information

The value **1em** is the current font size. Numbers below 1 reduce the font size, numbers above 1 increase it. The unit **em** allows decimals to be used rather than just integers.

Finally, we will declare a minimum height for the sidebar so that it will expand to house additional content, but will never contract below a certain height on the page. This will give us the flexibility of being able to grow the content without diminishing the element on the page visually – a terrific compromise.

Setting sidebar properties (cont.)

1 Open the HTML file you created in the previous task in your text editor and save it with a new name.

2 Open the style.css file in your text editor and locate the rule for the `<aside>` element.

3 Edit the rule by removing the declaration for the border.

4 Change the margin declaration to `margin: 0 0 0 2%;` to set the top, right and bottom margins to 0 and the left margin to 2 per cent.

5 Change the background colour from 'darkgray' to 'silver'.

6 Add a font size declaration to set the font size to `0.8em`.

7 Add a declaration for the line height, using the `line-height` property with the value `150%`.

8 Add the `min-height` property to the rule with the value `500px`. This is the minimum height setting, which is now set to 500 pixels.

```
70  aside {                    2
71  float:right;
72  margin: 0 0 0 2%;      4
73  padding: 0 20px;
74  background-color: silver;   5
75  color: black;
76  font-size: 0.8em;       6
77  line-height: 150%;     7
78  min-height: 500px;      8
79  }
80
81  aside > h2 {            9
82  background-color: silver;  10
83  color: black;
84  padding: 0;
85  margin: 0 0 10px 0;    10
86  }
```

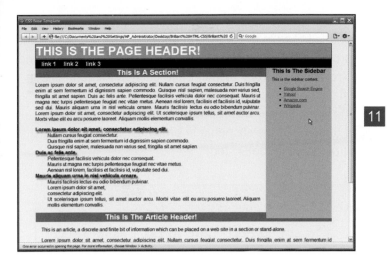

11

9 Locate the rule for the `<h2>` element in the `<aside>` element.

10 Change the background colour to 'silver', the padding value to '0' and the margin declaration values to '0 0 10px 0'.

11 Save the style sheet and load the HTML file in your web browser to view the results.

Cleaning up text and adding white space

This task introduces no new properties. We will simply open up the white space in the body content of the page and make it more professional in appearance. We'll remove the background colour from the `<body>` element and change the font colour to a softer grey to make the page less stark. While we're adjusting white space, we'll remove the indenting that we applied to some of the elements in previous tasks and centre the text of the page footer, too.

1 Open the HTML file from the previous task in your text editor and save it with a new name.

2 Locate the `<img>` tag in the HTML file and remove it, then save the HTML file again.

3 Open the style.css file in your text editor and locate the `<img>` tag. Remove it.

4 Locate the `<body>` rule and add a `line-height` declaration to the line height to '150%' and the font colour to '#666'.

5 Locate the `text-shadow` property in the `<dt>` tag rule and remove it.

6 Locate the `<section>` rule and remove the `margin` property, then add the value `article` to the selector. Be sure to separate the selectors with a comma.

7 Delete the `<article>` rule entirely, then add a second `<section>` element rule with only the `section` selector and set the width property to '80%'.

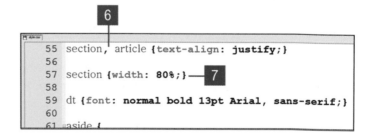

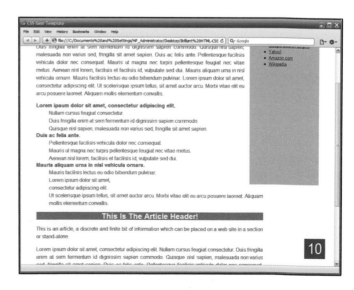

Congratulations! You've created a sharp, professional web page using only HTML5 and CSS3 for the most part. Of course, there are many more things you could do with it and, as you become more familiar with web design and programming, the sky is the limit in terms of what you can achieve with your web page designs.

To publish your page on the Internet requires a lot of research. First, you need to find a web host, but, don't worry, the Internet won't leave you to your own devices. Spend some quality time doing research on various hosting companies using search engines such as Google, Bing and Dogpile and you'll be sure to come up with a solution which fits your needs and budget. You might even discover many web hosting companies include content management systems (CMS), such as Joomla! or WordPress, which means you won't even need to write your own code. All you'll have to do is adjust what they provide to your tastes.

Having the skills to read, write and edit HTML and CSS code, though, will be of benefit to you whether you choose to create new web pages from scratch, maintain pages created by others or work with CMS platforms. Whichever way you go, I wish you success and hope this book has been of some benefit to you. I certainly enjoyed writing it.

Cleaning up text and adding white space (cont.)

17

8 Add the `text-align` property to the `<footer>` rule for the page and set the value to 'center' and reset the font size property (in the `font` declaration) from 'x-small' to '0.8em'.

9 For the final touch, add the `display: block;` property to the `<header>` element rule to correct the appearance of the header in the Opera™ browser.

10 Save the style sheet and load the HTML file in your browser to see the results.

Appendix 1

List of HTML tags used in this book

Tag	Function
`<a>...</a>`	Specifies an anchor on a web page. The anchor links to a document or other resource on the same page, in a new document on the same site or on a new site. The `href` attribute is required to specify the destination.
`<area>...</area>`	Specifies a portion of an image to be used as a hyperlink. The `href` attribute must be included in order for it to be a hyperlink.
`<article>...</article>`	Creates an HTML article division on the site, web page or in an HTML document.
`<aside>...</aside>`	Creates an HTML sidebar on a web page or in an HTML document.
`<b>...</b>`	Specifies content to appear bold.
`<blockquote>... </blockquotc>`	Specifies a longer section quoted from another source in HTML, to appear as a block, indented. Used with the `cite` attribute to link the quote to its source address, if available.
`<body></body>`	Specifies the body of an HTML table.
` `	Specifies a line break in content.
`<button>...</button>`	Specifies a button for an HTML form. The type of button it is is specified using the `type` attribute and the text content captured in the element is used as the text alongside the button itself.
`<caption>...</caption>`	Designates the title of a table, which is its parent element.
`<cite>...</cite>`	Specifies the name of a cited source, such as an author, book title, journal, article. Not to be confused with the `cite` attribute of the HTML `<quote>` and `<blockquote>` elements.
`<code>...</code>`	Specifies content as computer code.

Tag	Function
`<dd>...</dd>`	Specifies a definition, description or value for a term or name in a description list.
`<del>...</del>`	Specifies text to be shown as deleted, with a horizontal line through it. Also known as strikethrough.
`<dl>...</dl>`	Creates a description list, a definition-style list.
`<!DOCTYPE.../>`	Specifies the document type declaration.
`<dt>...</dt>`	Specifies a description term or definition term.
`<em>...</em>`	Specifies content to be emphasised or stressed.
`<fieldset>...</fieldset>`	Groups a set of form controls together under a single name.
`<figcaption>...</figcaption>`	Designates content which is used as the caption for a figure. The **`<figcaption>`** element must be either the first or last child element of the **`<figure>`** element. Only one figure caption is permitted per figure.
`<figure>...</figure>`	Designates content which is represented as a figure and referred to in the main content areas. A 'figure' can be textual content or an image, video or other media content.
`<footer>...</footer>`	Creates an HTML footer section on a web page or in a **`<section>`** or **`<article>`** element.
`<form>...</form>`	Specifies an HTML form. Several available attributes are used to specify the functionalities of the form itself.
`<h1>...</h1>`	Specifies a top-level HTML heading.
`<h2>...</h2>`	Specifies a second-level heading.
`<h3>...</h3>`	Specifies a third-level heading.
`<h4>...</h4>`	Specifies a fourth-level heading.
`<h5>...</h5>`	Specifies a fifth-level heading.
`<h6>...</h6>`	Specifies a sixth-level heading.
`<head>...</head>`	Specifies an HTML document's header section or element.
`<header>...</header>`	Creates an HTML header section on a web page or in a section or an article element.
`<html>...</html>`	Specifies the HTML markup portion of a document.
`<i>...</i>`	Specifies text content which is offset from the rest of the content to signify an alternative mood, voice or other factor. This was formerly the italic element and still italicises text.

Tag	Function
`<img>...</img>`	Specifies the location of an image on a web page. The `src` attribute is used to specify the location of the image file. The `width` attribute specifies the image's width, while the `height` attribute specifies its height. The `alt` attribute provides alternative text in the event the image can't be viewed.
`<input />`	Specifies an HTML input control. The input tag is an empty tag – that is, there is only one tag used, which is similar to the `<img />` tag.

`<input />`	Specifies an HTML control. The `type` attribute can be set to indicate the type of control to use. HTML5 specifications define the following new types of input controls:
	
	`email`
	`tel`
	`url`
	`number`
	`range`
	`date`
	`month`
	`week`
	`time`
	`datetime`
	`datetime-local`
	`search`
	`color`
	`checkbox`
	`radio`
	`password`
	`file`

`<ins>...</ins>`	Specifies inserted content.
`<label>...</label>`	Specifies a label for an HTML form object.
`<legend>...</legend>`	Provides the name and label for a group of control elements in a `<fieldset>` element.
`<li>...</li>`	Creates an item in an ordered or unordered list.
`<map>...</map>`	Specifies an image map. The `<img/>` tag's `usemap` attribute must match a hash name in the `name` attribute of a `<map>` element.

Tag	Function
`<nav>...</nav>`	Creates an HTML site navigation division.
`<ol>...</ol>`	Creates an ordered list, with numbered list items.
`<optgroup>...</optgroup>`	Groups a series of options presented in a user interface, together, under a common label.
`<option>...</option>`	Provides a list of options for various HTML controls.
`<p>...</p>`	Creates an HTML paragraph from text content.
`<q>...</q>`	Specifies a short, inline quote in HTML. Used with the `cite` attribute to link the quote to its source address, if available.
`<samp>...</samp>`	Specifies content as sample computer code.
`<section>...</section>`	Creates a section in the body of an HTML document.
`<select>...</select>`	Specifies a selection list or dropdown menu box. The `size` attribute specifies how many list items to display.
`<small>...<small>`	Specifies text which is displayed smaller than the surrounding text.
`<strong>...</strong>`	Specifies text which has strong importance for the content.
`<sub>...</sub>`	Specifies text to be displayed as subscript.
`<sup>...</sup>`	Specifies text to be displayed as superscript.
`<table>...</table>`	Specifies an HTML table.
`<tbody>...</tbody>`	Specifies the body of an HTML table.
`<td>...</td>`	Signifies an HTML table data cell.
`<textarea>...</textarea>`	Specifies a text area field – a field capable of holding far more text data than a `text` type field.
`<tfoot>...</tfoot>`	Designates a row or group of rows as the table footer section in an HTML table.
`<th>...</th>`	Designates a header cell within a table row.
`<thead>...</thead>`	Designates a table row or group of rows as a table header.
`<title>...<title>`	Specifies the HTML document's title.
`<tr>...</tr>`	Signifies an HTML table row.
`<ul>...</ul>`	Creates an HTML unordered list, where the items are not numbered but bulleted.
`<var>...</var>`	Specifies the enclosed content as a variable.

Appendix 2

List of CSS properties covered in this book

Property	Function
background-attachment: fixed	Specifies a background image does not scroll with a page, but a fixed background.
background-attachment: scroll	Specifies a background image scrolls with the page.
background-color	Specifies an element's background colour.
background-image: url(path)	Specifies a background image for an element.
background-position:	Specifies a background image's position on the page.
background-repeat: no-repeat	Specifies a background image does not repeat.
background-repeat: repeat	Specifies a background image is tiled.
background-repeat: repeat-x	Specifies a background image is tiled horizontally.
background-repeat: repeat-y	Specifies a background image is tiled vertically.
border	Sets the border for a selected element. Uses the settings for size, line style and colour.
border-image	Points to the image to be used and sets out how it is to be spread over the selected element's border. Requires the `url` setting and four image 'slice' sizes to apply the image to the border. Also requires the `repeat` type used for the image between corners to be set, to `none`, `stretch`, `round` or `repeat`. Use this in conjunction with the `border-width` property.
border-radius	Sets the radius of the rounded-off corner for the selected element's border in pixels. This property requires all four corners be set consecutively with no comma separators (`border-radius: 20px 20px 15px 15px;`, for example).

Property	Function
border-top-width border-right-width border-left-width border-bottom-width	Sets the border width in either pixels or as the values `thick`, `thin` or `medium` for a selected element.
border-width	Sets the width of a border for the selected element in pixels or as `thin`, `medium` or `thick` fixed values.
Both	Specifies floated elements may not float to either the left or right of an element.
clear	Specifies one or both sides to which other floated elements may not be set.
color	Specifies an element's foreground, or text, colour.
display	Specifies how to display an element. There are many choices, including `block`, which displays the element with a line break before and after it as a block-level element, and `inline`, which does not include a line break before and after the element and displays it as an inline element.
float	Specifies an element should be placed to one side or the other of all other normal-flowing elements.
font	Sets the family, style, weight and size all in one declaration.
font-family	Specifies the font family to be used. The font family can be either a specific family name or a generic font family.
font-size	Specifies a font's size.
font-style	Specifies the font's style to be normal, italic or oblique.
font-style: italic	Specifies a font's italics style.
font-style: normal	Specifies a font's normal style.
font-style: oblique	Instructs the browser to slant a font's normal style.
font-weight	Specifies a font's weight.
height	Specifies an element's height, in either relative or absolute units.
Inherit	Specifies an element inherit its containing ancestor's float value.
Inherit	Specifies the block-level element inherits its containing ancestor's clear value.
Left	Specifies an element float to the left of other normal-flowing elements.
left	Specifies no floated elements may float to the left of an element.

Property	Function
letter-spacing	Specifies space added between letters.
margin	Specifies an element's margin.
margin-bottom	Specifies an element's bottom margin.
margin-left	Specifies an element's left-hand margin.
margin-right	Specifies an element's right-hand margin.
margin-top	Specifies an element's top margin.
None	Specifies an element does not float.
none	Allows elements to float to the left or right or both sides of an element.
padding	Specifies all four sides of an element's padding in a single statement.
padding-bottom	Specifies the padding at the bottom of an element.
padding-left	Specifies the padding to the left of an element.
padding-right	Specifies the padding to the right of an element.
padding-top	Specifies the padding at the top of an element.
position: absolute	Specifies the absolute positioning of an element on a web page.
top	Specifies the distance from an element's top edge to the containing element's top edge.
right	Specifies the distance from the element's right edge to the containing element's right edge.
left	Specifies the distance from the element's left edge to the containing element's left edge.
bottom	Specifies the distance from the element's bottom edge to the containing element's bottom edge.
position: fixed	Specifies an element's position is fixed relative to the browser window. The position is not impacted by scrolling or window size changes.
bottom	Specifies an element is positioned up from its normal position.
left	Specifies an element is positioned to the right of its normal position.
right	Specifies an element is positioned to the left of its normal position.
top	Specifies an element is positioned down from its normal position.

Property	Function
position: relative	Specifies an element is positioned relative to its normal position by a browser.
bottom	Specifies an element is positioned up from its normal position.
left	Specifies an element is positioned to the right of its normal position.
right	Specifies an element is positioned to the left of its normal position.
top	Specifies an element is positioned down from its normal position.
Right	Specifies an element float to the right of other normal-flowing elements.
right	Specifies no floated element may float to the right of an element.
text-align: center	Specifies text is centred.
text-align: justify	Specifies text is justified.
text-align: left	Specifies text is ranged to the left.
text-align: right	Specifies text is ranged to the right.
text-decoration: blink	Specifies text to blink.
text-decoration: line-through	Specifies text has a line through it, as if it's been crossed out. Also called strikethrough.
text-decoration: none	Specifies no text decoration.
text-decoration: overline	Specifies text has a line above it.
text-decoration: underline	Specifies text is underlined.
text-indent	Specifies size of the indent for text.
text-shadow	Specifies the distance down and to the right the text shadow is to extend. It requires a colour for the shadow be indicated, by hexadecimal number or name.
text-transform: capitalize	Specifies the first letter of every word is a capital.
text-transform: lowercase	Specifies text is in lower case.
text-transform: none	Specifies no text is transformed.
text-transform: uppercase	Specifies text is in upper case.
width	Specifies an element's width, in either relative or absolute units.

Property	Function
word-spacing	Specifies space added between words.
z-index	Specifies the layering level of an element. The values are `auto`, which uses the same layer level as the parent element, and an integer. The higher the integer, the higher up the stack the element is layered.

Appendix 3

CSS colour names and numeric values

For one of the most exhaustive lists of CSS colours and their numeric values available, visit
www.somacon.com/p142.php.

Colour name	Hexadecimal value	RGB value
aliceblue	#f0f8ff	240,248,255
antiquewhite	#faebd7	250,235,215
aqua	#00ffff	0,255,255
aquamarine	#7fffd4	127,255,212
azure	#f0ffff	240,255,255
beige	#f5f5dc	245,245,220
bisque	#ffe4c4	255,228,196
black	#000000	0,0,0
blanchedalmond	#ffebcd	255,235,205
blue	#0000ff	0,0,255
blueviolet	#8a2be2	138,43,226
brown	#a52a2a	165,42,42
burlywood	#deb887	222,184,135
cadetblue	#5f9ea0	95,158,160
chartreuse	#7fff00	127,255,0
chocolate	#d2691e	210,105,30
coral	#ff7f50	255,127,80
cornflowerblue	#6495ed	100,149,237
cornsilk	#fff8dc	255,248,220
crimson	#dc143c	220,20,60
cyan	#00ffff	0,255,255

Colour name	Hexadecimal value	RGB value
darkblue	#00008b	0,0,139
darkcyan	#008b8b	0,139,139
darkgoldenrod	#b8860b	184,134,11
darkgray	#a9a9a9	169,169,169
darkgreen	#006400	0,100,0
darkgrey	#a9a9a9	169,169,169
darkkhaki	#bdb76b	189,183,107
darkmagenta	#8b008b	139,0,139
darkolivegreen	#556b2f	85,107,47
darkorange	#ff8c00	255,140,0
darkorchid	#9932cc	153,50,204
darkred	#8b0000	139,0,0
darksalmon	#e9967a	233,150,122
darkseagreen	#8fbc8f	143,188,143
darkslateblue	#483d8b	72,61,139
darkslategray	#2f4f4f	47,79,79
darkslategrey	#2f4f4f	47,79,79
darkturquoise	#00ced1	0,206,209
darkviolet	#9400d3	148,0,211
deeppink	#ff1493	255,20,147
deepskyblue	#00bfff	0,191,255
dimgray	#696969	105,105,105
dimgrey	#696969	105,105,105
dodgerblue	#1e90ff	30,144,255
firebrick	#b22222	178,34,34
floralwhite	#fffaf0	255,250,240
forestgreen	#228b22	34,139,34
fuchsia	#ff00ff	255,0,255
gainsboro	#dcdcdc	220,220,220
ghostwhite	#f8f8ff	248,248,255
gold	#ffd700	255,215,0
goldenrod	#daa520	218,165,32

Colour name	Hexadecimal value	RGB value
gray	#808080	128,128,128
green	#008000	0,128,0
greenyellow	#adff2f	173,255,47
grey	#808080	128,128,128
honeydew	#f0fff0	240,255,240
hotpink	#ff69b4	255,105,180
indianred	#cd5c5c	205,92,92
indigo	#4b0082	75,0,130
ivory	#fffff0	255,255,240
khaki	#f0e68c	240,230,140
lavender	#e6e6fa	230,230,250
lavenderblush	#fff0f5	255,240,245
lawngreen	#7cfc00	124,252,0
lemonchiffon	#fffacd	255,250,205
lightblue	#add8e6	173,216,230
lightcoral	#f08080	240,128,128
lightcyan	#e0ffff	224,255,255
lightgoldenrodyellow	#fafad2	250,250,210
lightgray	#d3d3d3	211,211,211
lightgreen	#90ee90	144,238,144
lightgrey	#d3d3d3	211,211,211
lightpink	#ffb6c1	255,182,193
lightsalmon	#ffa07a	255,160,122
lightseagreen	#20b2aa	32,178,170
lightskyblue	#87cefa	135,206,250
lightslategray	#778899	119,136,153
lightslategrey	#778899	119,136,153
lightsteelblue	#b0c4de	176,196,222
lightyellow	#ffffe0	255,255,224
lime	#00ff00	0,255,0
limegreen	#32cd32	50,205,50
linen	#faf0e6	250,240,230

Colour name	Hexadecimal value	RGB value
magenta	#ff00ff	255,0,255
maroon	#800000	128,0,0
mediumaquamarine	#66cdaa	102,205,170
mediumblue	#0000cd	0,0,205
mediumorchid	#ba55d3	186,85,211
mediumpurple	#9370db	147,112,219
mediumseagreen	#3cb371	60,179,113
mediumslateblue	#7b68ee	123,104,238
mediumspringgreen	#00fa9a	0,250,154
mediumturquoise	#48d1cc	72,209,204
mediumvioletred	#c71585	199,21,133
midnightblue	#191970	25,25,112
mintcream	#f5fffa	245,255,250
mistyrose	#ffe4e1	255,228,225
moccasin	#ffe4b5	255,228,181
navajowhite	#ffdead	255,222,173
navy	#000080	0,0,128
oldlace	#fdf5e6	253,245,230
olive	#808000	128,128,0
olivedrab	#6b8e23	107,142,35
orange	#ffa500	255,165,0
orangered	#ff4500	255,69,0
orchid	#da70d6	218,112,214
palegoldenrod	#eee8aa	238,232,170
palegreen	#98fb98	152,251,152
paleturquoise	#afeeee	175,238,238
palevioletred	#db7093	219,112,147
papayawhip	#ffefd5	255,239,213
peachpuff	#ffdab9	255,218,185
peru	#cd853f	205,133,63
pink	#ffc0cb	255,192,203
plum	#dda0dd	221,160,221

Colour name	Hexadecimal value	RGB value
powderblue	#b0e0e6	176,224,230
purple	#800080	128,0,128
red	#ff0000	255,0,0
rosybrown	#bc8f8f	188,143,143
royalblue	#4169e1	65,105,225
saddlebrown	#8b4513	139,69,19
salmon	#fa8072	250,128,114
sandybrown	#f4a460	244,164,96
seagreen	#2e8b57	46,139,87
seashell	#fff5ee	255,245,238
sienna	#a0522d	160,82,45
silver	#c0c0c0	192,192,192
skyblue	#87ceeb	135,206,235
slateblue	#6a5acd	106,90,205
slategray	#708090	112,128,144
slategrey	#708090	112,128,144
snow	#fffafa	255,250,250
springgreen	#00ff7f	0,255,127
steelblue	#4682b4	70,130,180
tan	#d2b48c	210,180,140
teal	#008080	0,128,128
thistle	#d8bfd8	216,191,216
tomato	#ff6347	255,99,71
turquoise	#40e0d0	64,224,208
violet	#ee82ee	238,130,238
wheat	#f5deb3	245,222,179
white	#ffffff	255,255,255
whitesmoke	#f5f5f5	245,245,245
yellow	#ffff00	255,255,0
yellowgreen	#9acd32	154,205,50

Jargon buster

Anchor A special hyperlink which contains an `href` element specifying another section of the same document.

Aspect ratio The ratio of width to height for a visual element, such as a video or image.

Attribute A specific property of an HTML element which alters how it is displayed or how it behaves. HTML element attributes are included in the start tag of the element.

Child element An HTML element which is nested inside another HTML element and containing content directly related to the *parent* element.

Code In the context of this book, this means computer programming, scripting or markup languages, such as JavaScript, HTML or CSS (Cascading Style Sheets).

Codec Software or a device which allows digital video or multimedia files to be played by manipulating a datastream (by encrypting, decrypting, compressing or decompressing, for example).

Column spanning Crossing over multiple columns in a table with a single data cell.

Combinator CSS code operators which are placed between simple selectors to allow granular selection of elements for formatting on a web page.

Controls Objects on an HTML form which receive inputs or settings from a website's users. Controls include objects such as dropdown lists or selection menus, 'radio' or option buttons, tick boxes (also called checkboxes), text fields, areas and more.

Disabled When a field or control on an HTML form, or a section of a form, is not available for users to interact with. Generally, certain conditions must be met or data provided to enable the disabled control(s).

Extension The three-digit part of a filename which follows the dot – 'filename. doc', for example.

Focus Placing a field or form control in the state of being ready for input. When the cursor resides in or on a form control, the control is said to 'have [the] focus'.

Hotspot A clickable section of an image or object on a web page. Clicking the hotspot triggers an event of some kind – usually a navigational hyperlink to another resource or section of the current resource.

HTTP header A digital 'tag' which is applied to a digital packet to enable it to be transmitted across the Internet.

Image map An image divided into clickable areas, or hotspots, which often function as navigational links to other resources or sections of a resource.

Inheritance When one object or element receives its properties or behaviours from a previously existing one, usually as a result of being nested within it.

Inline style A CSS style which is applied directly to the line or element it will affect.

Integer A whole, non-fractional, non-decimal number.

Left-aligned Text is ranged left with a ragged (or unjustified) right margin.

Legacy Older versions of software or hardware which must be accounted for in web design. An example of a legacy browser is Internet Explorer 6.0, which is still in use at the time of writing in some organisations.

Line break The end of a line of text, either as a result of encountering the page margin or by manual insertion of a line break, such as a carriage return on a manual typewriter or pressing the **Enter** key on a computer keyboard when using word processing software.

Metadata Information, or data, about data. This is information *about* a web page rather than *on* a web page. For example, a library catalogue is metadata because it describes publications.

Option button A 'radio' button which is not declared by the `<option>` element but, rather, by the `<input>` element using the `type` attribute to specify 'radio'. This is not to be confused with the `<option>` or the `<optgroup>` elements.

Option element An HTML control which provides list items for other `<select>` element controls.

Option group A group of `<option>` elements presented under a common label.

Parent element An HTML element which contains other directly related HTML elements and content, which are known as *child* elements.

Placeholder text Text which appears in a form field as a descriptor until the user enters the field for the purpose of data entry. Placeholder text can be anything and is often used to specify the type of information the user is required to input.

Row spanning Crossing over multiple rows in a table with a single data cell.

Simple selector The portion of a CSS rule which selects the element to be formatted. Simple selectors select only one element at a time without targeting their parent or child elements.

Subscript Text which is lowered beneath the line of text slightly and reduced in size. Subscript text is used in notation for chemicals, such as H_2O.

Superscript Text which is elevated above the line of text slightly and reduced in size. Superscript numbers are often used to indicate footnotes and in mathematics, measurements and so on to indicate a number is squared or to the power of, such as $2m^2$.

Syntax The rules for the appropriate use of components, whether computer or linguistic in nature, so a cohesive language and grammatical structure are formed. How components of a language of any kind are used to create the proper elements of the language.

Tabular data Data which is presented in table format – that is, in a series of rows and columns.

Troubleshooting guide

URLs and hyperlinks

Image handling

Working with HTML tables

Creating HTML forms